shown

THE

D0101402

CRIME INVESTIGATED

HAROLD SHIPMAN

THE DOCTOR OF DEATH

igloobooks

364. 1523

igloobooks

Published in 2014
by Igloo Books Ltd
Cottage Farm
Sywell
NN6 0BJ
www.igloobooks.com

Written by Mel Plehov

HUN001 0214
2 4 6 8 10 9 7 5 3 1
ISBN 978-1-78197-959-4

Printed and manufactured in China

contents

introduction

Harold Shipman

Introduction

Harold Shipman is one of the most understated, yet prolific, serial killers in history. He is associated with more than 250 murders, all taking place in a small area of northwest England; he worked and murdered in Hyde, a mill town in Greater Manchester. Revered and highly respected by his patients, no one had any idea of his dark motives and devastating crimes that went on, unnoticed for over 20 years. An active member of the community, Shipman blended in like a wolf in sheep's clothing – attending village meetings, sitting on local committees and organizing charity events. His patients spoke of his empathy and excellent bedside manner, of how he was kind, attentive and always had time for them. Yet underneath the benevolent exterior, he was fast-becoming Britain's most prolific serial killer with every single one of his victims known to him and placing their trust in his hands.

On 7th September 1998, the UK and the rest of the world were shocked and appalled as the news of Shipman's arrest broke and the full horror of his crimes came to light. The doctor, a well-respected member of the local community, had finally been discovered for the silent serial killer that he was.

As police continued to investigate past cases of suspicious deaths and began to look into Shipman's life, they uncovered some disturbing patterns around the unusually high death rate among his patients.

Dubbed the 'Doctor of Death', the ensuing investigation and trial held Shipman accountable for 15 deaths between 1995 and 1998. Shipman had abused his position as a revered healthcare professional to gain the trust of vulnerable, older women. Whether he had an 'angel of death' fixation, a 'God complex' or just a sadistic desire he had to sate, the trial revealed how he had killed his own patients with lethal injection of diamorphine.

Despite consistently protesting his innocence, the evidence against him was as compelling as it was disturbing and had it not been for discrepancies discovered in his last victim's will, who knows how long his killing spree might have lasted?

Eventually convicted and sentenced to life imprisonment, the sheer horror and extent of his crimes were yet to be revealed. A long and exhaustive public inquiry followed; commissioned by the British government and chaired by Dame Janet Smith OBE, the inquiry began in 2000, two years after Shipman was caught, and lasted until 2005, with its finding being released in various stages.

And although Shipman was convicted of just 15 murders, the inquiry later suggested that he could potentially be responsible for 250, if not more, deaths – Shipman's murderous activities had begun earlier than anyone had ever suspected. Escalating from his first kill, more victims fell each year. The true number of victims to fall foul to Shipman's lethal injections may have been even more than 250. Consisting of over 2,000 witness statements and accounts, together with in-depth analysis of nearly 300,000 pages worth of evidence, the six stages of the final report cost the taxpayer over £20 million.

The inquiry sought to answer the question on everyone's mind following Shipman's arrest – how did he get away with it for so long? Shipman's actions revealed major flaws in the health system that placed too much trust and a lack of accountability on General Practitioners.

Shipman's crimes can now be traced back to 1971, when he first began working at Pontefract General Infirmary. As well as the 250-plus deaths that investigators were able to attribute to Shipman, unconfirmed statements and stories from inside Preston Prison suggest that he may have been accountable for almost double the amount of deaths and perhaps not just of those who were elderly and infirm.

Even after he was incarcerated, there was one final act of violence Shipman was able to commit – fashioning a noose from his own bed sheets, the disgraced doctor took his own life on the 13th of January 2004, the day before his birthday. And just like all of the other lives he took, nobody could have predicted his intentions until it was too late. Only earlier on that same day, he had seemed happy and cheerful and chatted on the phone to his loyal wife, Primrose. Listening back to the recording of the call, there was no inkling of what he was about to do.

Many questions about Shipman's life and atrocities remain unanswered and the following chapters will delve into the life of Britain's most infamous serial killer. This in-depth account will investigate how he committed his crimes, how he was able to get away with it for so long, his early life and influences and the question on everyone's mind, the answer to which we may never know – why?

Chapter 1

The Truth Comes Out

The Truth Comes Out

No one knew what Shipman had been doing as the body of Kathleen Grundy, his final victim, was pulled from the ground. But Britain was soon to discover the full extent and horror of what he had done. It would later be revealed that he had systematically killed at least 250 people over his career, with a great many more suspicious looking deaths in his shady history as well.

Shipman's life of crime suddenly began to unravel in August 1998 when suspicions into the death of Kathleen Grundy led to a gruesome, late-night exhumation in a dark cemetery. A team of police officers and gravediggers began digging up the corpse of the recently deceased 81-year-old widow from Hyde. Her gravestone read, 'Died Unexpectedly After A Lifetime Of Helping Others'.

Despite the hour, a crowd of onlookers had gathered to watch as the coffin was winched out of the grounds of the graveyard behind Hyde chapel. Little did they know at this point, that Kathleen Grundy was the latest victim of Hyde's very own 'Doctor of Death'.

Detective Inspector Egerton watched on, the reality of what he ordered dawning on him and his officers. It's not every day you get permission to exhume a body for an investigative autopsy and although he had evidence to back up his suspicions it was still a major undertaking. Accusing a well-respected doctor, a pillar of the community, of murder was a big deal and something the police needed to be 100% sure on.

As events unfolded, the hunch would pay dividends and Kathleen Grundy's exhumation would be the key turning point that ended the killing spree of Dr Shipman.

Kathleen Grundy lived in Gee Cross, one of the oldest areas of Hyde. It is a picturesque village on the edge of the Peak District, set atop a valley that leads into the bowl of Manchester city centre. Married to the former mayor of Hyde, Kathleen had been a widow for 20 years after her husband died suddenly of a heart attack. Despite being 81, she was described as active and mobile and regularly attended village events. She was a member of several societies, including the pensioners' lunch club – a volunteer-led community group that she helped to run.

During the week leading up to her death she had been as active as usual, embarking on a coach trip to Derbyshire with a group of friends, as well as volunteering in the local Age Concern shop, which was situated, quite ironically, opposite Shipman's surgery. Even the day before her death she had been out visiting friends. Her mind was as sharp as ever as she commented on current affairs, analysed the World Cup football match and Wimbledon Tennis Tournament as well as speaking about her family and sharing her grandson's successes proudly with the group. All of these factors meant her imminent death would be most unexpected and rang alarm bells in the minds of her family and close friends.

On Wednesday 24th June 1998, Grundy had failed to attend one of her usual events and so two friends went to her house, also known as Loughrigg Cottage, to check if she was all right. John Green, the caretaker of the pensioners' club and Ronald Green, a fellow volunteer made the journey to her house. Kathleen had many friends in the village who looked out for her, carried her bags, offered her lifts and visited regularly. But when her friends arrived that morning, something was wrong: usually tight on security, Grundy's front door was open and unlocked – this was odd because not only was it usually locked with two bolts, this door wasn't often used by Kathleen as she preferred to come and go through the back door, using the gate at the side of the house.

Upon entering the house, John and Ronald made the horrific discovery – their friend lay dead on her sofa. She was fully clothed and curled up in a sleeping position – her body cold to the touch and her skin an ashen grey. As a close-knit community, the friends' first instinct was to call Dr Shipman, a trusted doctor and known by many as Grundy's GP.

It didn't take long for Shipman to arrive on the scene, flaunting his power and authority as a GP to pronounce Kathleen dead and to even propose the cause of death. Shipman revealed to the men that he had seen Kathleen earlier that morning 'for a chat' and that she must have been well enough to clothe herself. The men reported that the doctor, who carried out a perfunctory examination, stated the cause of death was 'cardiac arrest'.

Not used to dealing with death, the two friends were unsure of what to do next and so consulted Dr Shipman, asking his advice on how best to proceed. Shipman said that they should contact her solicitors at a law firm in Hyde, Hamilton Ward; it may have seemed strange at the time that Shipman knew who her solicitors were, but the men trusted their local doctor and followed his instructions. The solicitors very quickly advised Grundy's friends to get in contact with her immediate family, particularly her next of kin. However, they were unable to reach Grundy's daughter, Angela, and so the police were called as a last resort. Police officers were sent to Grundy's house; they then spoke to her GP – Dr Harold Shipman. When speaking to the police, Shipman offered a more vague explanation for her death than he had previously stated to John and Ronald – natural causes.

The police were able to track down Kathleen Grundy's daughter, Angela, who now lived in Warwickshire. They spoke on the phone and broke the news of her mother's sudden and tragic death. Angela was in a state of shock, having only spoken to her mother a couple of days prior to her death, she couldn't understand how her health had deteriorated to such a critical point. There had been no precursor or underlying medical conditions; a devastated Angela and her husband, David Woodruff, set off for Hyde first thing the following morning.

After arriving in Hyde, Angela met with Dr Shipman to discuss the circumstances of her mother's death. Just like he had told John and Ronald, Shipman recounted his earlier visit to Kathleen, adding that he had indeed seen her the day before for a 'routine check'. In Angela's recollection from her meeting with Shipman, she recalls that he had seen Kathleen the morning of her death and implied that she had been complaining of feeling unwell – a story that contradicted what he had told John and Ronald when he was called to Grundy's body the day before. Angela recalls Shipman's persona being somewhat cold and unsympathetic, completely unlike the character he had been described as by Kathleen and other members of the Hyde community. He suggested to Angela that the cause of Kathleen's death was simply 'old age'. In fact – that is what Shipman had chosen to put on Grundy's death certificate; a cause which is usually only used by doctors as a last resort, when patients are clearly suffering or old and infirm, it would not be used when patients were active and thriving just days before death. This diagnosis did not sit right with Angela, nor with other doctors who were consulted. In fact, old age is usually only cited as a cause of death if followed up with medical evidence of severe bodily function failures. However, because Doctor Shipman (a supposed medical professional) had attended Kathleen hours before and then just after her death, his word was not questioned and the cause of death was registered.

But for Angela, the real shock came a few days after the funeral, when she learned of her mother's will. A solicitor herself, Angela had helped her mother with her will and knew that she had wanted to bequeath her estate and any money evenly amongst her surviving family members. Surprisingly, only days before her death, Kathleen Grundy had apparently altered her entire will – writing a letter and enclosing a new will and testament that excluded her entire family and left everything she owned to Dr Harold Frederick Shipman.

For both Angela and Grundy's solicitors, alarm bells were ringing. And stranger still another letter arrived a few days later from someone by the name of Smith, claiming to have helped Grundy type out her new will and also informing the solicitors of her death. Hamilton Ward solicitors knew better than to act on a £400,000 estate based on instructions from two anonymous, typewritten letters and so they tracked down Angela, sending her copies of her mother's new will. Immediately, things did not add up for Angela. The will was oddly worded, vague and included spelling mistakes, which Angela stated would have been out of character for her mother, who was meticulous when it came to spelling and grammar.

Angela continued to investigate the dubious will herself, first attempting to find the mysterious typist known as 'Smith', but to no avail. Next, she set out to find the people who had supposedly witnessed her mother's signature and new will. The two witnesses' names were Paul Spencer and Claire Hutchinson. Neither were particularly hard for Angela to track down as both were local to the area; Paul even worked in a pet shop close to Shipman's surgery.

Angela first tracked down Claire, asking her if she remembered signing a will. Hutchinson knew nothing of Grundy's will, but did remember signing something in the surgery. Spurred on to find out more, Angela visited Paul at the pet shop and listened as he recounted how Shipman had manipulated both himself and Claire into witnessing life-changing legal documents without raising the slightest hint of suspicion. Paul remembered how he had been sat in the GP's waiting room, waiting to see the doctor for a repeat prescription of antibiotics. He recalled details about Shipman's character, how he was genial and always made an effort to remember little details about each patient, so as to make them feel cared for. Whilst he was waiting, Claire Hutchinson was also sat in the doctor's waiting room. Shipman causally popped his head around the corner and asked if they wouldn't mind witnessing a signature. Perhaps because of his casual nature and perhaps because of his respected position as a long-standing family doctor, neither Paul nor Claire were suspicious and followed Shipman into his room. Inside, Kathleen was already there and answered an emphatic "Yes" when Shipman asked her, "Are you sure?" Shipman then presented both Claire and Paul with a doubled over form and asked them to print, sign and write down their addresses. It appears both witnesses signed the document without asking what it was or checking, and then thought nothing more of it. Had Shipman deliberately preyed on Paul and Claire knowing they would be easily swayed into being unknowing conspirators in his evil plan? Or, had he become so blasé and confident that he had the trust and respect of an entire community that he simply asked whoever he spotted in the waiting room that morning? Perhaps he had got away with his crimes for so long that he had delusions of grandeur – who would dare question him, surely any document present by a doctor would be taken at face value as credible?

For Angela, the pieces were beginning to slot into place. Could it really be? The gravity of what she was thinking may have held her back this far, but spurred on by her suspicions, she investigated the dubious will even further, cross-checking her mother's signature from the deposits she made on behalf of 'Age Concern' against the signature on her will. By this point in her investigations, it probably came as no surprise that the signatures did not match. In a press interview, Angela also recalled her mother talking to her about a survey that Dr Shipman had asked her to participate in, a survey about aging that was being conducted at Manchester University. Police later suspected that Shipman had created a bogus form for this survey, which would enable him to obtain her signature as well as two witness signatures – pointing to a cold and calculating mind. It would later be revealed that Shipman already knew how and when he was going to kill Kathleen Grundy. Her death was no accident, but a premeditated murder.

It must have been hard for Angela to believe, that her mother's own doctor would be responsible for killing her and now she would have to convince the police of this too.

Angela Woodruff voiced her concerns to the police and on 31st July 1998, DI Egerton and DC Dave O'Brien began the investigation. At first glance, it was clear to both officers that they were obviously dealing with a case of fraud. Because Kathleen Grundy's estate consisted of two houses as well as bank accounts and a lump sum payout from a recent sale of a third house, all of which amounted to nearly £400,000, this was a serious crime in itself.

The case of the fraudulent will would, in the end, be Shipman's downfall and there is much speculation over why he took such a risky move, a move that would clearly attract attention and put him under scrutiny. Some researchers suggest that he had grown tired of the killings and because he was a pathological serial killer, he couldn't simply stop – he would have to be stopped. Such a brazen display of arrogance and by shining the spotlight on his activities was a sure-fire way to be found out. However, others suggest that he may have been planning for his retirement, since he was nearly the age of 60.

Perhaps he had become over-confident – having got away with serial killings without the slightest hint of detection, his arrogance may have been his undoing; perhaps thinking his position as a respected doctor somehow placed him above questioning and above suspicion. Either way the case of Kathleen Grundy's fraudulent will sparked a series of memories and suspicions in the mind of the investigating officers on the case…

… A previous police investigation implicating Dr Shipman was recalled, and on record were statements from a different practicing GP in the area alerting the coroner to the unusually high death rate amongst Shipman's patients. With this seemingly one-off accusation, Shipman's involvement in the fraudulent will and the unexpected nature of Kathleen Grundy's death, a disturbing and terrible possibility was dawning on those involved, including the police officers, the coroner and Grundy's daughter, Angela.

Having sought advice from his superiors, the grim realization of what he had to do next became all too apparent – he was going to have to exhume Kathleen Grundy's body. This decision was a pivotal moment in uncovering Shipman for the murderer that he really was. Shipman had thought ahead, pre-empting any such activity when he altered Grundy's will: in it he had typed out that she now wanted to be cremated instead of buried. Luckily, the final decision lay with the family; Angela, well aware that her mum had always wanted to be buried rather than cremated, followed these wishes. Besides, the new will did not indeed surface until after the funeral.

The exhumation took place in the dead of night; looking like a scene from a gruesome horror film, detectives, and even curious onlookers from the village, stood in the floodlit grounds of Hyde cemetery – driving rain adding atmosphere and causing the digger to slip in the wet mud. The coroner had made the potentially distressing decision to exhume based on information from the police, the dubious nature of Grundy's death and also because he remembered Shipman's name being implicated in a previous discussion about the alarmingly high death rate amongst his older patients. Despite the anguish an exhumation can cause a family, the coroner felt it was the right course of action – and to rule out any foul play a full post-mortem would need to be carried out.

It was this decision that would break the case and in the months to come, the police would look back and thank Angela Woodruff for her tireless detective work that grew from her mother's fraudulent will. Her personal investigations led her straight to Shipman, placing him at the centre. For his final victim, Shipman had made a mistake by preying on an elderly woman who was healthy and fit despite her aging years, a woman whose daughter was a solicitor and who kept in touch regularly. Unlike other victims, Grundy did not slip easily under the radar.

The exhumation took place on 1st August 1998, they began digging at 2am, hoping to be finished before sunrise. Present were a number of officials including crime scene investigators, known as SOCOs (Scene of Crime Officers). The police themselves were not able to exhume the body and it was left to a team of official gravediggers, presided over by the funeral director, his management team and a police photographer. The distressing scene unfolded before their eyes, no one ever having witnessed a real-life exhumation; surely this kind of thing only happens in gritty TV programs? The scene even sparked concern from onlookers who, unaware of the exhumation order, were horrified at the thought that some sick individuals were defiling a grave in their beloved town. No matter how subtle the investigators tried to be, they could not help but spark rumour and intrigue; in fact Shipman's name was already being mentioned in connection with Kathleen's death amongst the town folk.

The coffin was winched from the ground, soil samples and photographs were then taken before the oak casket was transported to Tameside General Hospital, where a post-mortem was to be carried out immediately. The forensic pathologist who carried out the examination was Dr John Rutherford. Little did he know at that time that this would be the first of many of Shipman's victims he would have to examine.

At the same time as the post-mortem took place, police obtained a search warrant and raided Shipman's house. Worried that rumours of the investigation would reach him, they acted quickly so that he would not have the chance to hide evidence. The police turned up towards the end of his surgery hours and escorted him back inside the building. They seized his typewriter and although seemingly unphased, Shipman confided in a colleague that he was 'in trouble'. While officers visited the surgery, more police visited his home in Roe Cross Green, intercepting any further chance Shipman might take to return home and destroy or remove evidence. Although the police did not find any 'smoking guns' at this point, they uncovered a home life situation out of control with mess and clutter everywhere. They noted stacks of confidential medical files just sitting around in his garage along with boxes as well as more files inside the house; they also noted large amounts of jewellery that they suspected did not belong to his wife, Primrose. At this point, Shipman appeared co-operative and friendly, even finding and handing over the typewriter he knew he had used to forge Grundy's will, telling police, "Kathleen Grundy borrowed it from time to time." Later, SOCOs would match Shipman's fingerprints to the typewriter and to the supposed will of Kathleen Grundy, however, none of Grundy's fingerprints were ever found on either the typewriter or the will.

Shipman was proactive, even holding his own press conference to deflect negative attention and suspicions. The press showed little to no interest with only the Manchester Evening News running a small story on the unusual events following the death of an old lady. The community rallied around Shipman, refusing to believe he could possibly have murdered his own patient and forged her will to disinherit her own family for his own financial gain. His supporters barely even raised an eyebrow, trusting their local GP so much that they did not even entertain the idea that he might be responsible for the death of an innocent old lady, a genuine pillar of their community.

A month after the exhumation of Kathleen Grundy's body, toxicologists were finally able to attribute a cause of death and it would send shockwaves through the community. Contradicting Shipman's earlier diagnosis of 'old age', the real cause of death was found to be a lethal overdose of morphine. Shipman had made a grave error in his method of execution – traces of morphine stay in the blood, skin, hair and organs for a long time, even after death so it was easy to identify that a large dose had been introduced into Kathleen Grundy's system and that the quantity involved would have resulted in death within two or three hours. The results were as shocking as they were decisive in the mind of the investigating officers – this had gone from a simple case of fraud to a murder investigation.

Of course, Shipman was well aware of what the toxicology reports would turn up and had pre-empted. Having access to all of his medical files and still working in his surgery, Shipman was able to falsify Grundy's notes, adding inserts into the margin suggesting that she was a drug addict. The police were obviously dubious and, had it not been for the seriousness of the alleged crimes, might have laughed in Shipman's face as he continued to imply she had an addiction to some sort of opiate. As well as adding hand-written notes to the margins of her existing notes, making sure the false observations dated back at least two years, he had also gone into her electronic files, adding extra, back-dated entries into the computer system, perhaps unaware that his electronic activity could be tracked.

Things didn't add up for the investigating officers, how could Shipman have been so clumsy with the forged will? And why chose a drug such as morphine to kill his patient, a lethal overdose of any number of other substances, such as ephedrine or even insulin, would have never been detected. The question posed by analysts looking back at this particular victim's case, was: had Harold Shipman become so arrogant that he'd developed a 'God complex' thinking his actions would not attract attention due to his social status? Or had he simply grown tired of the killings and, either consciously or subconsciously, wanted to get caught?

Five days after the results of the toxicology report, Shipman was brought in for questioning. Transcripts from the police interviews reveal Shipman's cold and calculating side, having thought of an explanation for all of the dubious events surrounding Grundy's will. He knew that it was his word against a scorned daughter and the flippant manner in which he spoke of the events, as if an everyday occurrence, revealed his confidence that he would soon be let out and free to go home. Soon, he realized his worst fears about the case, he was being accused of murdering Kathleen Grundy via a lethal injection of morphine. Although Shipman had prepared for this accusation and had already tampered with Grundy's medical files, he was not prepared for the depth of interrogation and research that the police would go into.

Shipman's entire defence was based on the assumption that Grundy was addicted to some sort of opiate: he suggested morphine, heroin and pethidine as likely examples. However preposterous the thought of an 81-year old woman injecting heroin, this was his story and he was sticking to it. He expected detectives to believe this based on his own observations, once again putting all of his faith into his status as a respected doctor. Shipman had breezed through the last 20 years of his career without suspicion, his medical opinions hadn't been questioned and he'd been able to literally get away with murder by abusing his position as a GP. For Shipman, this was likely the first time his opinion hadn't been readily accepted and now he was being forced to answer more and more intricate questions on the matter without preparation.

Of course, the police did not buy his story of an elderly, ex-Mayoress and active member of the community being a heroin addict. Shipman was about to be challenged once more. The police informed him that they had thoroughly searched Grundy's house and had found no evidence of drug use, no substances, paraphernalia or syringes. Furthermore, the dose required to kill her would have only been available from a heroin dealer or via a large prescription of morphine, something that would usually be administered in a hospital or via a district nurse. Had this been the case, surely there would have been evidence of packaging and a way in which she administered the drug to herself? Shipman was caught out in his lies once more; detectives had trawled through Grundy's medical records and with the help of analysts pinpointed the entries they believed to be false. Cross-referring the dates and times of the entries, they soon discovered that Shipman had been shopping with his credit card miles away from his surgery at exactly the same time he was supposedly treating Kathleen Grundy. The shopkeeper, who remembered Shipman fastidiously mulling over which pen nib to buy, taking time to try each nib until he eventually settled for a £140 fountain pen, confirmed the credit card transaction.

The police put it to Shipman that when he visited Kathleen Grundy on the morning of 24th June 1998, he did not take a blood sample, which is what he had told her he would be doing (and there has since been no evidence that a blood sample existed from that morning); instead he injected Kathleen with a lethal dose of morphine that would have knocked her unconscious and powerless to her fate almost immediately and would have killed her between ten minutes and three hours later.

Although he denied the charges, by the end of the day Shipman had been charged by police with the murder of Kathleen Grundy and also charged with fraud. Shipman was kept in custody overnight; a bail figure of £150,000 was set and friends and family rallied together to raise funds for his release. However, their efforts were to no avail – Shipman appeared at Tameside magistrates' court in Ashton-under-Lyne and was officially charged with murdering Mrs Grundy and forging her will. He was refused bail.

This moment marked the beginning of the end of Shipman's secret murders. As news broke, the community of Hyde was shocked and appalled, a well-respected and cherished member of their community since 1970 was a murderer. He had a reputation as the best and most trusted doctor in the area, he had the biggest patient list and a waiting list for more, many of whom were, ironically, elderly woman who had heard such good reports about his kindness, competence and benevolent manner. Many did not, and could not, believe Shipman would commit such a crime and the surgery was inundated with cards and messages of support. Many of those offering their support would later find out that Shipman had murdered an elderly and vulnerable member of their own family.

But for the police this was just the beginning. The questions that had been raised some years ago about Shipman's unusually high and ultimately unknown death count were brought to the fore once more. Could it be that this was not just a one-off case? Over the course of the next two weeks, police delved into the recent deaths recorded by Shipman and instantly noticed a high number of causes listed simply as 'natural causes' or 'old age'. It became all too apparent that Kathleen Grundy may not have been Shipman's only victim. At this point Detective Superintendent Bernard Postles became more involved in the case. The police were stood on the precipice of breaking possibly the biggest serial case in British history. Just how many people had Shipman killed? And how far back did his crimes go? Postles has been quoted as saying that what they were about to embark upon could be bigger than anything anyone had ever investigated before, or probably ever would.

Chapter 2

Early Life

Early Life

Shipman was the middle child in his family; his mother doted on him but also had very high expectations. His early academic career was built on trying to impress his mother and her death was a huge turning point in his life. Many criminologists believe that his mother's death was the catalyst for his pathological behaviour that led to so many killings.

Harold Frederick Shipman was born on the 14th January 1946. He would have been one of the first babies of the baby-boomer era. His parents, Harold and Vera Shipman married in 1937 and had a child, Pauline, just before the outbreak of World War II. Harold (senior) worked in a hosiery factory, which was a common industry in their hometown of Nottingham. Vera was just eighteen when she married Harold; a year later their first child, Pauline, was born in 1938. Not long after this, early on in the following year, Harold was sent away to war after joining up to the Sherwood Foresters regiment, as the family lived in the Sherwood area of Nottingham, which is approximately five miles north of the city.

Harold (junior) was born just eight months after the end of World War II, he soon became known as Fred to his friends and family, as using his middle name saved confusion between his and his father's name. His brother, Clive, was born four years later. The three Shipman children were brought up through fairly humble times. Their parents worked hard to provide for them and Vera, especially, instilled discipline and manners into the children; friends and co-workers reportedly described the Shipman children as 'a credit to Vera', who ran a tidy home and brought up her children with good morals.

Fred Shipman's childhood home was a three-bed terrace on Longmead Drive. Ostensibly, they were a normal family who were not too overprotective, but were close-knit. The siblings shared a healthy, loving bond – particularly Fred and his older sister. Pauline, being seven years older, would dote on Fred and help her mother run the household. However, it was clear to neighbours that Harold and Vera, perhaps Vera in particular, thought of their children as different and special. They perhaps wanted a better life for them than the working class life they had experienced themselves. Harold senior certainly didn't want his sons working in a factory for their entire life. This superior attitude became apparent to neighbours, who noted that the Shipman children were not like the rest of the children on the street – they didn't mix or socialize and certainly didn't play in the street with the other children very often. The Shipman children had quite an insular upbringing, only really being influenced by parents and schooling. Some might suggest that this kind of upbringing led the Shipman children to believe that they were somehow better than those around them. When Brian Whittle, a key researcher into Shipman's life, went back to Nottingham to interview residents of Longmead Drive who might remember him, they remembered 'Fred' or 'Freddie' always being on the outskirts; if he came out to play, he would have to go home early, or wouldn't join in with play fighting and other boyish behaviour – he was never considered 'one of the lads', in part due to his absence and in part, due to his nature.

Fred was the middle child and several researchers report that his mother, Vera, focused the most attention on him – she viewed him as the bright spark in the family, the one who would go far. For school and family photos, she always would dress him in starched and ironed shirts, neat trousers and either a tie or bow tie. Fred had few friends growing up; most people speak of how he kept to himself and usually hung around with the same small group of friends. Whittle met with an old school friend, Bob Studholme: Bob recalled that he would always be 'on the fringe', choosing not to get too involved or emotionally attached to anyone. Fred played on school sports teams, but chose not to get involved with the usual changing room banter and boyish behaviour. Old school 'friends' recalled him being present but not fully engaged in whatever activity was happening.

Fred passed the 11-plus entrance exam and attended the prestigious High Pavement Grammar School, Nottingham. His parents, especially Vera, were extremely proud – he was on the path to success. But this was a double-edged sword: because of the distance away from their home, Fred would have had to get up early every day to make the long commute to school, before long days of intensive lessons, in classes where he was no longer the brightest child. He was gifted in some aspects, such as science and sport, but even then he had to work hard to keep up with his classmates. Researchers and criminal profilers alike suggest that Fred worked so hard, not for himself, but to please his mother, who had such high expectations of him.

Fred's strong relationship with his mother shaped his character. In school he struggled with English, but persevered, knowing how important gaining basic qualifications in English and maths would be. In classes he would rarely contribute or join in debates, instead he chose to listen and observe others. Where he excelled most was on the rugby pitch. He played for both his school and at county level, and, despite his aloof persona, he was not afraid to get stuck in and take tackles for the benefit of the team. Rugby brought out Fred's competitive nature and his desire to be superior. Friend's recall how he would turn into a machine on the pitch, quite the opposite of his quiet, introverted persona off the pitch. When facing the opposition, he would target his player and make sure he came out on top. Fred was also a keen cross-country runner and friends remember him always toeing the line, being careful not to get caught breaking any school rules, and certainly not joining in when others cut corners or made cheeky stops along the route. He was never in detention and although he knew how to be sociable, he wouldn't join in with any tom-foolery or rule-breaking that might end up disappointing his beloved mother.

Fred matured early; going through puberty fairly young made him the envy of many of his classmates. He grew sideburns and had to shave from the age of fourteen. Building muscle and the added testosterone helped his rugby career, but not his love life… Unlike many of his peers, Fred failed to woo any of the young ladies from the neighbouring sixth-form girls school, Manning. Instead, he took his sister to school dances, who must have stood out, being seven years his senior. The odd couple looked ridiculously out of place as they danced a jive they had practiced at home, his sister, towering above him in height.

Fred had a special relationship with his mother and this grew stronger as he got older and achieved more in school. He would forego playing with the lads in the street, who always assumed, quite rightly, that he was stuck indoors reading or doing homework. Vera made sure he had a peaceful environment in which to study. She pinned all her hopes on young Harold, as his older sister, Pauline, had left school at fifteen, working for a local wool manufacturer and his younger brother, Clive, had not been bright enough to make it into the same elite grammar school as Fred. Many profilers have related that the influence a strong matriarchal figure, particularly in the early stages of life, can have an effect on future serial killers; both Fred West and Dennis Nilsen (the Kindly Killer) had this in common with Harold Shipman.

And for Fred, tragedy struck when his mother was diagnosed with terminal lung cancer in 1963. It would have been a drawn-out and painful death, but the family kept these experiences private, with school friends and colleagues having no idea of the gravity of Vera Shipman's illness.

During his mother's illness and deterioration, it would have been Shipman that predominantly cared for her. His father would have been out working hard, providing for the family and his sister would, too, have been working long hours. As such, the young Harold Shipman would be the first to return home to his ailing mother. He soon settled into a routine of making her comfortable and bringing her tea whilst they waited for the doctor to arrive.

And it is this early experience of a visiting doctor that may well have shaped Harold's career, both as a doctor and a serial killer. For Vera, relief came when the doctor would arrive with a regular dose of morphine, to ease the pain. Harold saw first-hand the positive effects of morphine; he would have witnessed the whole procedure from the doctor preparing the syringe to the injection and the ensuing relief and respite that it gave his mother.

Vera deteriorated as the cancer took hold, eventually becoming bed-ridden. During the weeks and final days leading up to her death, the afternoon doses of morphine became increasingly stronger and would be all Vera would look forward to, a relief from the agony and suffering. For Fred, witnessing his mother, who had doted on him for seventeen years, slipping away from him must have been terribly distressing.

It is not hard for criminologists to make the link between Shipman's chosen method for killing his patients and his early experiences with his dying mother. Although Kathleen Grundy was an exception to the rule, in regard to his killing pattern, it was later determined that he would even choose to administer his lethal doses of morphine in the afternoon – consistent with his mother's experiences. It is obvious what a huge influence his mother's death had on him, as well as his mother's almost overbearing affection and expectation that preceded it. Some criminologists go on to suggest that Shipman may have also got a buzz from seeing the power his local GP had. The control over life and death, pain and remission could have fascinated him. Indeed, his upbringing and schooling had already set him on a path of arrogance and superiority, so it is likely his motives for later becoming a doctor were more about superiority, control and sadism, rather than wanting to care for and help others.

For Shipman, morphine was the first real drug he was exposed to and he became extremely familiar and comfortable with it over the months leading up to his mother's death. It is easy to see why he went on to choose this particular drug as his weapon of choice – he knew all too well the effects and quantities needed. It was also a clean and peaceful solution to ending a life. This becomes even more apparent when learning that Shipman's mother eventually died on 21st June 1963 after falling into a morphine-induced coma. Fred was present as this took place and although it is impossible to either confirm or deny – it is quite likely that Vera's GP, Dr Andrew Campbell, would have discussed with the family and informed them that her suffering was such that she was unable to fight for her life any longer. Either acting alone, or with the family's consent, the GP would have given Vera a larger, lethal, dose of morphine – one that would have sent her into a peaceful, painless sleep and ended her life.

Whilst technically illegal, this practice is thought to be common amongst GPs dealing with terminally ill patients who are in endless suffering and exhausted physically and mentally, from the drugs and from fighting the cancer. Understandably, it is not something doctors will ever admit to or talk about on record, however, it does happen and is generally accepted amongst peers given the extreme circumstances. In fact, as news of Shipman's crimes initially broke, some, more trusting and understanding, medical professionals suggested this may have been the reason for Shipman's actions – that he was purely ending their suffering. However, this, of course, did not turn out to be the case.

His mother's death would have ignited mixed emotions inside the young and emotionally repressed Harold Shipman. To lose his mother would have been devastating, particularly at such a young age. However, the relief and release that would have followed that final dose of morphine would have also instilled a peace inside him that she was no longer in pain. And perhaps feeling relief at her death would have then led to feelings of anguish and perhaps even guilt. Conceivably, this inner turmoil may have led Shipman to seek out the peace he must have felt witnessing the pain leave his mother; perhaps his subsequent kills were a way to reconnect to that moment, to find that moment of peace once again?

Vera died on a Friday, and by Monday, Harold was back in school. He spoke little of his mother's passing, choosing to channel his grief into athletics. His school friends were shocked when the discovered the news and most only found out when he wore a black armband on his blazer on the day of her funeral. His emotional blankness in the face of such tragedy was possibly more shocking than the tragedy itself. No witnesses ever saw him shed a tear or even look sad. Instead he remained stoic and just 'got on with things'. This kind of emotional distancing could be attributed to many things, perhaps it was just his way of dealing with grief, perhaps he had undiagnosed tendencies towards autism or Asperger's syndrome, or more worryingly – it could point to psychopathy; a psychopath being someone who is incapable, or has a diminished sense, of empathy and remorse.

It was this early experience that first gave him a real insight into the medical profession; he may have already been thinking about it, or been pushed into it by his mother: either way it is clear he was set on this career path from the A-level choices he made (biology, physics and chemistry, despite having to work hard to understand and achieve good grades). And as he witnessed his local GP injecting his mother with such powerful drugs, being able to control her pain and eventually her life, who knows what the real motive for wanting to become a doctor really was?

Even in the 1960s, medicine was a popular career and the young Harold Shipman, despite his hard work and hours of study, failed to get good enough grades to get into his chosen medical school at Leeds University. Although he may not have shown it on the outside, it could have been that his mother's death affected him, and the disruption in home life combined with the raw grief at such a critical point in his development could have had a detrimental affect on his focus and eventual results. Or alternatively, he may not have been clever enough to handle three science A-levels plus all of the extra lessons and sports commitments he took on throughout his sixth-form years. Of course, it is not a crime to be intellectually mediocre and average exam results would not usually be a talking point. However, when juxtaposed against his later arrogance and the way in which he lorded his intellectual superiority over people – it is an interesting discovery.

However, his mother's influence and wishes for him to be a success were strong and he re-took his A-levels in November 1964. Having to take a year out of education before he could attend Leeds University Medical School in the autumn of 1965. Coming from a working-class background was advantageous for Shipman and his father's low-wage, now as a single parent, meant that he could attend the medical school on a full student grant – only available to those from the lowest income families. Plus, at that time, tuition fees were paid for by the government – perhaps this situation added towards Shipman's sense of entitlement and superiority, receiving special treatment even then.

Leaving home would now be a lot easier for Harold. The wrench from his mother, had she still been alive, would have been hard. However, since her death, his home environment would not have been the same. Doted on by his mother, he was not necessarily the favoured child by everyone else – Pauline, his older sister, was working a full time job and taking over many household duties previously carried out by Vera. His father, Harold continued to work long hours and helped Pauline to run the home. Clive was moving forward with his own life, pursuing a career as a health inspector.

Shipman started medical school in September 1965, opting to share a house with a fellow student instead of living in halls of residence provided by the university. Although still a difficult profession to enter, becoming a doctor was not like the competitive environment today. The government was crying out for new medics to come through the ranks. There was a severe lack of doctors and nurses throughout the NHS, particularly GPs, with many GPs around the country having more than the maximum limit of 3,500 patients on their lists. Shipman's mother would have been extremely proud of his success thus far, having groomed him from a young age to make something of himself, to escape the working-class lifestyle that she and her husband had experienced.

For Shipman, this may have been a turning point in his life, the transition from a boy weighed down by expectation and academic pressure to a young man about to embark upon a highly respected career that would no doubt leave him in a comfortable financial position in life. But it was during his time in Leeds that other, life-changing events would take place. The first of which was when he met a young girl by the name of Primrose.

Chapter 3

Primrose

Primrose

Primrose Oxtoby became Shipman's wife and loyal companion to the bitter end. Primrose was Shipman's first ever girlfriend and he was her first ever boyfriend. Primrose shared her entire life with Shipman, even working at his surgery in Hyde, yet she has always denied knowing anything about the murders. Sometimes, she was even present when Shipman visited the dead bodies of his victims.

Harold Shipman met his future wife whilst in his first year of medical school at Leeds University. Harold and his housemate would regularly catch the same number 38 bus as a young girl by the name of Primrose Oxtoby. Primrose would later become Shipman's loyal wife and change from the giggling girl at the back of the number 38 bus, to the sour-faced, overweight woman who attended Shipman's every court hearing, standing by her husband and denying any knowledge of any of his sick crimes.

Primrose was born to George and Edna Oxtoby in April 1949, and named Primrose-May because of the flowers and blossom that bloomed during the month of her birth. Primrose was a late addition to the Oxtoby family, being thirteen years her sister's junior. Her parents were nearing middle age when she was born. Primrose would later speak about how her parents had really wanted a boy, not another girl, and that the significant age gap between herself and her sister made for a lonely existence growing up. Her strict, conservative upbringing could be attributed to the fact that her parents were older when they had her, they hailed from a previous generation with slightly different morals and she may have lived a more old-fashioned way of life, growing up, compared to her peers.

Like Shipman, Primrose was from a working-class background; she grew up in the village of East Rigton, near Wetherby, West Yorkshire. Edna, her mother, was a good housewife, running a clean home and looking after her family while George, her father, worked on a local farm. Although George was the bread-winner, it was clear that Edna wore the trousers at home.

Primrose attended the local primary school in Bardsey and like Shipman, her upbringing was also quite insular. Her religious mother did not see any value in play or children's social events because she could not understand what the benefit might be, or perhaps more likely, she did not want Primrose to be influenced by children raised in much more relaxed homes. As such, Primrose did not play with the other children in her village.

As well as schooling, Primrose learnt the piano, was made to attend church, Sunday school and even bible classes. Her strict Christian upbringing was important to Edna, who regularly quizzed her daughter on her biblical knowledge. She was not allowed to attend the local youth club or socialize too late at night. However, as she grew older and transitioned into a teenager and was exposed to more external influences, she was bound to rebel.

Primrose's only escape from her overprotective mother was the Girl Guides. She joined from a young age and rose through the ranks, eventually being trusted to take younger girls on a hiking trip through the Yorkshire Dales.

Unlike Shipman, Primrose did not take an 11-plus exam and was not fortunate enough to benefit from a grammar-school education. Like other children from her village, she attended Wetherby Country Secondary School. Without the opportunities of a grammar school, Primrose's path in life was already set to be a more mediocre one than

Shipman's and although there would have been the option to transfer to a college in order to obtain qualifications, Primrose, like most of her school friends, left education at fifteen with no O-levels, or CSEs.

So, at the tender age of seventeen, she was working her first real job as a window dresser, having flunked out of school without any notable qualifications. All was not lost on that front, however, because Primrose had a talent for art and creativity and had won a competition and through it gained a place on an art and design course in Leeds city centre. The college course led to the window dressing job and this meant she wound up on the same bus at the same time as the young Harold Shipman.

In 1965, both Harold and Primrose bore little resemblance to the pictures shown in the media coverage following his arrest and subsequent trial. At that time, Shipman was a tall, dark and handsome young man. He was well built and lean from his athletic pursuits, he had a full head of dark hair and a promising future as a doctor – he would have been quite a catch. Former classmates described Primrose as 'well-built, but not fat'; she had a short bob hairstyle, but that was as the only aspect of her that fitted into the youth culture that epitomized the swinging sixties. She dressed conservatively, perhaps due to her religious upbringing, and showed little interest in drinking, drugs and partying.

No one knows exactly how they got together, perhaps they saw each other on the bus several times, or perhaps it was love at first sight. It is clear Harold had a confidence that had been lacking in his sixth-form days when the only girl he could get to go to the school dance with him was his sister. They began to chat on their bus journeys into town and, after weeks of no more than smiles and small talk, Harold finally plucked up the courage to ask her out on a date.

It's quite likely that Shipman was the first person to show an interest in Primrose. Throughout school she had been plain and unremarkable, attracting no attention from the boys. Some researchers put it down to her conservative and socially restrictive upbringing, whilst others might suggest it was not all to do with her upbringing – perhaps she was just a 'plain Jane'. However, a year at college and girly influences may have helped Primrose come out of her shell.

Shipman took Primrose to a coffee shop in Leeds and they must have hit it off straight away. It wasn't long before they were officially an item. Shipman was Primrose's first (and only) love and she fell head over heels for the young, would-be doctor. Investigators who spoke to Shipman's fellow students from that time remember how excited they both were to be in a relationship – perhaps both pleased that they had finally managed to get together with someone of the opposite sex. Shipman introduced her as his girlfriend very quickly and she went along to student functions and parties, although she failed to make much of an impact with her dowdy looks and lower IQ compared to Shipman and his peers.

By the time Shipman had just turned twenty, and Primrose was still seventeen, she fell pregnant. Commentators on Shipman's life have looked back at this moment and wondered, had she not fallen pregnant, would he have stayed with her? At that time, Primrose was below Shipman's league in terms of looks and intellect. It's hard to understand how the two were compatible and perhaps something we will never find out. And although Shipman was regarded as handsome in his youth, he was still inexperienced in love and had a track record of being socially awkward and aloof. Some might wonder if he chose Primrose as an easy target, someone he could feel superior to and feel secure in a relationship, knowing that she adored him. Geoffrey Wansell, a journalist researching Shipman's case, believed that Primrose actually suffered from a rare psychological condition called 'Folie à Deux', which is when two people who have a close relationship (usually living together), share a psychosis, in which a dominant partner makes the submissive partner accept their delusions and value system. Wansell suggests that Harold Shipman – acting like a sorcerer – groomed his barely literate wife into believing his own fantasies and thereby turned her into his greatest ally. He is not, of course, suggesting that she knew of his crimes, just that he was able to act however he liked, knowing he would not be questioned by his submissive partner.

When she learnt that she was pregnant, Primrose was, in fact, excited at the prospect. Given her strict religious upbringing and the length of time she had known Shipman, one would assume she might have been worried or anxious about the situation. However, in 1965, abortions were not legal and so there were not many options available to the fledgling couple. Although Shipman's reaction to the news is unknown, investigator Carole Peters, reported an alleged conversation Shipman had with a nursing colleague where he alluded to the pregnancy being a mistake and that he should have known better. This is all speculation of course and whether Shipman was as invested in the relationship as Primrose will remain a cloudy area, perhaps even to Primrose herself.

Harold and Primrose had two choices – keep the baby, or give it up for adoption; either way, their parents were going to find out about it. First, Primrose told her friends, who were the same girlfriends who had caught Shipman's eye on the number 38 bus (these were friends Primrose had made after starting art college and getting her design job, friends her mother did not entirely approve of). Needless to say, both sets of parents were horrified, fearing the worst for the young couple.

Shipman's father and his older sister were disappointed by his behaviour and his stupidity. Perhaps Harold was secretly relieved that his mother was no longer around, knowing how much the news would have upset her. Having worked his whole life, thus far, to please his mother, she would have been turning in her grave at this news. His family worried for his future medical career, wondering if having two dependants whilst going through the rigours of medical school would be too much for the same boy that had to retake his A-levels after flunking under pressure the first time around.

Primrose's parents were devastated. They had protected her from the evils of the world for so long and it appeared that she had gone off the rails after being given the tiniest hint of freedom. Having a teenage daughter pregnant out of wedlock would bring shame on the family and offended their Christian beliefs. Harold had no choice – he would have to marry Primrose.

The thought of their daughter marrying a would-be doctor, someone on the path to success and riches, should have been a comfort to the Oxtoby's. However, Edna, in particular, took an instant dislike to Harold Shipman. It could have been the case, that when faced with such life-changing news, much like the news of his mother's death, Shipman detracted from the situation emotionally; Either not knowing how to act about the situation, or simply not feeling anything in the first place. So, although Shipman looked good on paper, his demeanour and arrogance even shone through at this early stage.

The marriage of Harold Frederick Shipman to Primrose-May Oxtoby was a pathetic affair; held in the local register office with minimal fuss and away from their local community (Edna did not want the shame of someone seeing her daughter getting wed with a visible baby bump). The two fathers bore witness to a particularly understated and unenthusiastic ceremony. None of their friends attended the wedding and no one has ever found photos of the day's events.

During his second year at college, Harold was able to get a small flat for him and his new wife. The flat was more convenient for Harold, being close to the medical school, but was far away from Primrose's parents in Wetherby. Primrose continued to work as a window dresser until she was physically too big to perform the role any longer. At such a young age, Shipman had tied himself down to a life of domesticity, unable to join in with the usual student activities; instead he had to come home to his heavily pregnant wife after long days of lectures and practical sessions. He had, indeed, made a rod for his own back.

Primrose lived in Shipman's student flat until a few weeks before she was due to give birth. Unfortunately, Shipman was not made welcome in the Oxtoby household, even though he was Primrose's husband. Shipman would have found this perturbing to say the least, having grown up being the favoured child, been successful in sports and accepted by his peers at school, he was not used to meeting with people's disapproval or disdain. But instead of trying to ingratiate himself with Primrose's parents, Shipman instead chose to remove himself from the situation opting not to visit Primrose at home and instead made her meet him somewhere close, like a café or a pub.

Only a few months into their married life, the Shipmans' first child was born. Sarah Rosemary Shipman was born on 14th February 1967 at Harrogate General Hospital. Unfortunately for Shipman, things were about to get worse. Once Primrose had left her job, the couple only had his student grant to survive on. The £340 a year was barely enough for a student to live on, let alone a young family, and so Harold and Primrose had to rely on Primrose's parents for financial support. It is quite likely that this scenario would have irked Harold. Being supported by people he considered to be beneath him socially and, what's more, by people who openly disliked him.

Harold must have felt a certain degree of bitterness at the way his life was shaping up. Having left a house of sadness and pain following his mother's tragic death, he had briefly entered a new world full of possibilities and opportunities – yet he had fallen at the first hurdle, becoming so caught up in the idea of having a girlfriend and finally losing his virginity that he lost perspective, either through ignorance or exuberance, and now found himself in a potentially hopeless situation. An arrogant and self-centred man, this feeling of being trapped in a life he didn't choose could have been building on the foundations of underlying dark urges to kill. His opinion of himself compared to his real-life situation was a complete contradiction, and unable to act out against it (for fear of losing face, or of jeopardising a career he'd worked his whole life for) he may have repressed these feelings of resentment to resurface at a later date. In fact, this theory has been backed up by several criminologists who believe that huge internal trauma combined with external social pressures can lead to violent and aggressive tendencies – combine this with the calculating and repressed emotions of a psychopath, and you may have a recipe for murder.

Wansell's 'Folie à Deux' diagnosis was seeming to fit Primrose's behaviour more and more. Unlike most eighteen-year old girls with a new-born baby, she seemed to enjoy being tied down and having her freedom restricted. She had been brought up helping her mother and older sister to run the house and so took to her new role as a subservient housewife like a duck to water. Former peers of Shipman, when interviewed later in life, remember his house being unlike those of fellow students – it was more homely and settled and Primrose, whilst still failing to make an impression with her personality, was always on hand to provide guests with tea and other refreshments. This obsession with being the dutiful wife and making everything perfect fits with Wansell's theory.

In fact, Wansell goes further, comparing Primrose and her character to that of Rosemary West, wife of the famous serial killer Fred West. Like Primrose was to Shipman, Rosemary West was also Fred's intellectual inferior. Just like Primrose, she too denied any knowledge of her husband's murderous behaviour, despite Fred West's killings taking place in her own basement. Just like Primrose, Rosemary met her future husband on a bus (but when she was just fifteen), and only months later she was pregnant with his child – the similarities are eerie. And just as Primrose had an overbearing mother, Rosemary was the daughter of a protective and controlling father. The two submissive wives both went on to have large families with their murderous husbands, perhaps feeling this to be the ultimate form of affection – having their husband's children were like a personification of their love.

Wansell believes that psychopathic killers like Shipman and Fred West are subconsciously drawn to women they can dominate – that their submission indulges their fantasy of control and feeds their over-inflated ego. Imagine how differently Shipman's life could have been if he had met a woman who called him out on his controlling behaviour, who questioned where he was going and what he was doing and who didn't put him on a pedestal? Perhaps he would have been more humble, learnt to accept criticism and not develop a 'God complex', and maybe, just maybe, he may not have fed his desire to kill and kill again.

Shipman continued to live in his student flat with Primrose, juggling the pressures of medical school and a new family as best he could. From the outside he looked in control, happy; but inside he was unravelling, harbouring feelings of bitterness and resentment, perhaps feeling like he'd been dealt a raw deal. And it would be many years until he no longer had to struggle on through life; but through thick and thin, Primrose stood by Harold, hanging on his every word, making his every wish her command. It may have been accidental, but Shipman had found the perfect partner, someone who would allow him to commit his heinous crimes without question or obstruction.

Chapter 4

Medical School

Medical School

Some commentators believe that Shipman may have started killing as early in his career as medical school. It is known that he learnt about, and experimented with lethal drugs – including opiates – during his time at medical school. Shipman started taking Pethidine at this time, a dangerous addiction that almost led to his downfall many years later.

In the autumn of 1965, a young Harold Shipman arrived in Leeds, ready to take the first step in his medical career. Leeds University Medical School was his first choice place of study and he had wanted to go there so much that he had taken a year out to redo his A-levels, having not performed well enough the first time to secure his place. To attend a lesser college, or switch to a different career choice was not an option for Shipman. His mother had high hopes for him; he was the favoured child in the family and the only one of his siblings likely to achieve a better quality of life and break away from the Shipman family's working-class background.

Just like it is today, choosing medicine meant signing up for one of the hardest degrees you can do. It meant five years at university, followed by a year working in a hospital to gain vital experience. It would be six years at least until Harold would have the power he craved so much, and it would be many more years until he would be able to act autonomously and without question.

During the 1960s, university populations experienced a boom, possibly the start of the baby-boomer generation coming through, or perhaps due to higher standards of education beginning to take form across the UK, with more children from working class backgrounds, like Shipman, being given the opportunity to attend a grammar school that, in previous generations, would have been a closed door to them. Because of the high influx of students, Leeds did not have enough spaces in their various halls of residence to accommodate all the students. For Shipman, this meant he would have to live in a house further away from the university. The university had appealed for families with spare rooms to offer up their homes to new students and these 'approved residencies' were then doled out to the unlucky 'Freshers' that did not get into university halls. Shipman and another student were farmed out to a house on the Wetherby road, a twenty-minute bus journey, plus a short walk, away from the medical school. And it was on this bus journey, of course, that he would meet Primrose.

Like many other academic institutions during the 1960s, Leeds University was a hotbed of new ideas and revolution. Students campaigned for equality and about various social issues, but Shipman would have little time to get involved with any of this. His lectures began at 8.30am and usually finished at 4pm, with only a short break over lunch. They would be intensive and intellectually challenging. Once again, Shipman found himself at the limit of his abilities – not known for his natural flair or particularly high IQ, he had got this far through hard work and perseverance – medical school would be no different. Even though Wednesday afternoons were free (a tradition at red brick universities that kept Wednesday afternoons free for sporting activities), medical students made up for this luxury by having to attend lectures on a Saturday morning instead.

For Harold, there was no chance of reliving his glory days on the rugby pitch. He was struggling to keep up. To make matters even worse, he was having to commute into Leeds from his student home near Wetherby, adding extra pressure to an already busy day. He had to work hard outside of lectures to make sure he was performing and understanding at the same level as his peers; this meant working evenings and weekends. Having a girlfriend added an extra time pressure for Shipman, and any time not spent studying was spent with Primrose – even before she was pregnant.

Medical school was not like embarking on a normal degree. It was, quite literally, a case of life and death if the students did not understand; and as such, Shipman and his fellow students were constantly quizzed and examined on every topic. As well as verbal quizzes, the students also carried out practical tests on each other, including blood tests and clinical studies on various drugs. Brian Whittle reports that one of the tests he would have taken part in would have been a placebo test involving morphine – with four students participating in a double blind test. Unlike most of his peers, Shipman had already had experience with morphine, during his mother's drawn-out death. Perhaps this was the moment where he suddenly realized the power he could have, should he become a qualified doctor. He had already seen the power of morphine and now he knew he would have the means to obtain it without drawing attention to himself. Perhaps the drug and its effects intrigued him, or gave him a buzz of some kind?

Harold's first year went smoothly enough, he had it all going for him – his hard work was paying off and he was keeping up in his medical degree; he had also managed to attract a female companion and maintain a relationship. He was coping well with the transition from home life to student life and everything was on track… until Primrose fell pregnant.

The news of Primrose's pregnancy may have rocked Shipman's perfect little world, but he did well to hide it. His already busy work schedule and meagre student grant of £340 per year was about to come under even more strain. He had no choice but to marry Primrose, and his time would soon be split three ways: university, wife and now – baby!

Early into his second year, his first child was born: Sarah Rosemary. Harold continued on with the next three and a half years of medical school and, like his school years, he was once again on the fringes – although this time it may not have been his preferred choice. Having a wife and child meant he was unable to join in the usual student activities such as drinking and socializing, playing sports and joining clubs and societies. Furthermore, his ego was being bruised from all angles: his peers were out-performing him, generally scoring higher marks and getting more answers right during tutorials; he was also having to be supported financially by Primrose's parents, who had taken an instant dislike to Shipman almost instantly. He may not have shown it on the outside, but it is quite likely that bitterness, frustration and inner turmoil was bubbling away under the surface.

The structure of medical school at that time was two years of academic study, plus a further three years of practical work alongside more academic learning. The culmination of the first two years of a medical degree was a key time in any young doctor's career. It would lead to the first qualification on the road to becoming part of the General Medical Council (GMC). Shipman, predictably, did not achieve greatness. But this time he avoided the shame and embarrassment of having to resit his exams, scraping through and gaining his first medical qualification – an MB, Bachelor of Medicine.

The following three years of the course were more practical and hands on. Shipman would have to work closely with his peers on several projects and clinical tests, but because of his special home-life situation and his predisposition to remain on the fringes, he failed to make much of an impression on those he worked with. Luckily for him, he wasn't disliked, but he was not memorable either – perhaps something he later found useful for flying under the radar with his criminal tendencies.

The medical students would spend their time observing and being taught practical scenarios in teaching hospitals around South Yorkshire. The added travel, social pressure, time management and increasingly complex workload would have taken its toll on the young medic. The culmination of these three years would be an intensive and exhausting round of exams, known as 'Finals'. Final exams lasted about a month and were the hardest thing most of the students would have ever faced. The pressure to perform and to get a good grade (so as to secure a good placement the following year) was high. The end of the final run of exams would have exhausted most medics without commitments, let alone those trying to raise a baby and support a wife. The exam process may have seemed cruel and a lot of pressure to put people under; however, it was important to grill them, to really check that they understood and appreciated the responsibility that comes with being a doctor. Soon the fledgling doctors would be responsible for the lives of others – Leeds University could not risk gaps in knowledge or poor decision-making under pressure, given the seriousness of the job they were applying for.

Passing Finals meant the transition from student to junior doctor and with it came a provisional registration with the General Medical Council. By 1970, Shipman had endured a physically and mentally grueling five years of medical training. During this time he had also developed an addiction to pethidine (a drug that acts in a similar way to morphine). Once again, he managed to scrape by, gaining an unremarkable pass in all his examinations – placing himself well below his peers in terms of knowledge and achievement.

At the time, the next step after five years in medical school was to become a junior doctor, or a so-called junior house officer. For Shipman, having a wife and child had advantages, at least in terms of protecting his ego. Because, for most students, the aim was to secure a junior house officer position in city hospitals where the work was more exciting and life was more vibrant. However, this meant strong competition and only the graduates with the best results would be able to secure these positions.

Shipman may not have even considered this as an option. Instead he applied for a junior house officer position somewhere much more remote. He would have told colleagues, family, Primrose, and even himself, that the reason for this was that the more rural places offered better accommodation for doctors and their families. Applying to remote, unpopular locations meant that his mediocre results were less of an issue.

Harold was twenty-four when he moved to Pontefract General Infirmary with his wife and daughter. For the young family, the run-down and shabby accommodation provided for doctors was actually a step up for the Shipmans, who had grown used to living in Harold's tiny student flat. To them, the place was spacious and far more practical for raising a family. And it was a good job too, because soon after Harold passed his final exams, Primrose fell pregnant once again.

The accommodation provided was actually part of the hospital, and as such was perfect for Shipman and his hectic work life. Being a junior house officer is often described as the hardest year of a doctor's life. Fresh out of medical school, junior doctors were suddenly thrust into real life situations and were expected to take responsibility and make decisions. The hours were long and, to begin with at least, every case would have been a new, unprecedented challenge. From emergencies, to routine checks, everything and anything was expected of a junior house officer. But without completing yet another gruelling year, Shipman would not be able to fully register with the General Medical Council, he wouldn't be able to go any further with his medical career – for Shipman it was vital that he complete this year of training in order to gain the freedom to practice unsupervised.

The year of a junior house officer was split into two, six-month periods – one medical and one surgical. Throughout the year, Shipman would be monitored and supervised by a team of consultants. Yet despite this supervision, a number of mysterious deaths occurred that have since been, almost certainly, attributed to Shipman. It is clear that the title of doctor and the superior feelings he got from treating patients was building up inside Shipman. His confidence grew as he became the 'go to' doctor for nurses around the hospital. This may not have been due to his medical expertise, but more so because he spent many hours studying, either in the library or in the doctors' common room. With a child and a pregnant wife to care for, his salary did not stretch far and so, once again, he was ostracized from his peers, who chose to unwind in the local pub of an evening. He readily took on extra shifts to earn more money for his dependent family.

Some commentators suggest that the extra time and familiarity (due to his living situation) with the hospital may have led Shipman to feel over-confident in his position at the hospital. As a result the nurses, in particular, took a shine to him, perhaps because he was always available and had a deeper medical knowledge than them; they would have respected his decisions and trusted his medical opinions. However, colleagues on a similar or higher level than him had a different opinion – many found him aloof and anti-social, they described him as a loner and were confused by his confidence, possibly aware of his sub-standard grades at Leeds University Medical School. Unfortunately, Shipman's eagerness to get involved and find a solution was beginning to rub some people up the wrong way. For he had a tendency of never admitting he was wrong or at fault; it is likely that he would turn a simple differential diagnosis into a competition, a competition where he always had to be right.

Brian Whittle speaks of several early instances where Shipman's arrogance led to some compromising medical situations that, had they not turned out OK, could have resulted in a case of medical malpractice. In one instance, Shipman took it upon himself to defibrillate a patient, knowing full well that such a risky and important procedure should have been carried out by a consultant with a registrar assisting – definitely not a junior house officer acting alone. By all accounts, the consultant was livid with Shipman when he realized the horror of what he had done and what the disastrous consequences might have been. Shipman also raised suspicion when working one of his extra shifts on the Accident and Emergency Ward; whilst attending a patient, he knowingly administered a huge dose of diazepam (also known as valium, an opiate related to morphine) to a patient who had come in with a bad cut on her leg. The dose was only needed to calm her down and 5mg would have been enough. However, Shipman reportedly gave her 'almost four times' the normal dose, choosing to ignore words of warning from the nurse, who tried to tell him that he was giving the patient too much. Remembering this event, the nurse in question reported to Whittle that she remembered Shipman showing no signs of nervousness whilst administering the drug. Perhaps, even at this point, Shipman had more experience with opiates than he was letting on. He might have known exactly how much would be a suitable dose to calm her down, without sending her into a fatal coma, and not too much that, should she have an adverse reaction, he would be questioned too much.

It could have even been the case that Shipman was using these early patients to experiment with dosage, pushing the limits to find out how much might be needed to calm someone, knock someone out, comatose a person, and eventually kill them.

Getting away with minor crimes like these fuelled Shipman's arrogance; he was operating above the system, wielding his power as a doctor, even a junior one, without reprimand or consequence. He would have felt smug knowing he was getting one over on his superiors, people he considered to be beneath him, despite their higher status, and people who didn't deem him worthy of higher grades in his exams – he would show them who really was the top dog.

In society, Shipman was now also rising, feeling superior to the 'average Joe' on the street thanks to his qualifications and training. He would have been regarded as somewhat of a martyr, having willingly come to a small, limited town like Pontefract when he had been trained in the big city of Leeds, at one of the top medical schools. He was cementing his position as a 'top guy', a 'hard-worker', someone who was responsible and reliable, someone you could trust.

Towards the end of his year as a junior house officer, on 21st April 1971, Shipman's second child was born – Christopher Frederick Shipman. He was born in the same hospital that Shipman worked and lived in and was christened with the same middle name as his father.

As his confidence grew, juggling a young family and career in medicine became easier – more than likely aided by Primrose, who continued to support her husband, to cater to his every whim. He would always have food waiting for him and a clean and well-kept house. She would never question the extra hours he spent in the hospital and always believed that his medical opinion was above question.

A worrying combination of a growing ego, total adoration and support at home, as well as from the nurses, together with relative freedom on the wards meant Shipman was able to sail closer and closer to the wind, and it wasn't long before the death toll at Pontefract General Infirmary began to mount.

Chapter 5

Early Warnings and Addiction

Early Warnings and Addiction

During his time as a junior doctor at Pontefract General Infirmary, Shipman was most likely responsible for the deaths of at least three patients, including a young girl. There were eight more suspicious deaths and countless others signed off by Shipman. In his early career, there had been several reports of malpractice and strange behaviour, but none of them made it to his permanent record and Shipman was allowed to continue practicing medicine.

Shipman's early medical career was crammed full of exams, hours of endless study, hectic workdays and raising a young family. But he was also harbouring a dark secret, a deadly addiction that almost ended his career before it began. Shipman was somewhat of a control freak, always needing to be right and always having to appear like he was coping. Perhaps to deal with the huge amounts of stress he was under, or maybe even out of curiosity, Shipman turned to drugs.

His drug of choice was an interesting one – pethidine. Pethidine was one of the first opiate drugs manufactured for clinical use, and was seen in hospitals as early as the 1930s. Pethidine was generally used as a strong painkiller, the first choice for doctors whose patients were in a moderate amount of pain that could not be treated with the usual over-the-counter painkillers. During the 1970s, the height of Shipman's addiction to the substance, around 60% of doctors prescribed pethidine for acute pain and 22% for chronic pain. Nowadays it is rarely used, but back then it was commonly administered for managing post-operative pain and due to its added bonus of having anti-spasmodic, muscle-relaxing effects, it was widely used in obstetrics and gynaecology departments. It could then be suggested that it was no coincidence that Shipman chose to study for diplomas in child health (1972) and in obstetrics and gynaecology (1974); perhaps he was following the easiest path to acquiring pethidine without raising too much suspicion.

For Shipman, the misuse of this drug started way before he was a junior doctor, and was more likely taken up during medical school. Unlike other students, Shipman did not have extra money to spend on beer and socializing and so he needed another way to unwind, to deal with the stress. Since medics learnt the effects and advantages of various drugs, pethidine was not an uncommon choice for substance abuse. Shipman was probably not alone in his use.

It is unknown exactly when Shipman started taking drugs, could it have been as early as his second year when he was suddenly lumbered with a wife and child? Or might it have been later, after gaining access to medical supplies during placements, he might have seen an opportunity to acquire the drug and use it to help himself through his final exams. The drug had two very useful qualities: it numbed the senses allowing you to be calm in stressful situations, whilst it also stimulated the serotonin receptors in the brain which, in turn, created a mild sense of happiness (or euphoria). Many medical commentators have looked back and noted that pethidine was usually the narcotic of choice for overworked and stressed-out doctors. However, the most common abusers of the drug were actually midwives; pethidine was regularly prescribed to those suffering from the after-effects of childbirth and seeing the calming and euphoric effect, midwives would try it out for themselves. And although it has not been proven, many doctors also reported that the drug allowed them to concentrate and focus for longer through intensive days of work.

However, there is a fine line and misuse of an opiate can render you incapable of functioning, especially on a level where you are caring for the vulnerable and the sick.

It has been suggested from most sources that Shipman was definitely abusing pethidine during the run-up to his final exams and beyond. The fact that no one knows for sure shows that Shipman kept his addiction well hidden – even using powerful opiates, he seemed to be in control. Perhaps Shipman wasn't like most addicts, constantly chasing the feeling of the first high or needing to feed ever-demanding cravings. It has already been suggested that he had psychopathic tendencies, so forming an emotional attachment to the effects of a drug is a much more unlikely scenario than that of a well-adjusted person. His reasons for drug use could have been a pathological one – he had started a ritual and now needed to continue with it. Could this have been a pathology that escalated into a murderous pathology: once he had taken pethidine a couple of times and got away with it, he grew comfortable with the drug and continued to use it whether he needed to or not – later on, once he had taken a life or two and got away with it, perhaps he continued to do it purely to feed his morbid pathological condition.

When questioned later in life, none of his fellow medics remember him exhibiting any signs of drug addiction. He was able to hide it from his peers and supervisors, as well as obtain the drug without so much as raising an eyebrow of suspicion. Getting away with this early crime would have bolstered his ego, fuelling his arrogance and perhaps set in motion deadlier intentions – if he could get away with this, what else could he get away with?

Once Harold started working in hospitals, his access to pethidine became even easier. Pethidine, unlike morphine, was often needed to be prescribed in large doses. This is because it wasn't as powerful and although this might be considered a disadvantage, for doctors it meant that they could manage pain more effectively and safely. Prescribing even small, but regular, doses of morphine could easily lead to addiction and result in patients who couldn't function in their jobs or home life. On the flip side, pethidine was weaker – it didn't knock people out and actually helped some people function due to its euphoric effect. As a result, doctors would prescribe large doses of pethidine instead of small doses of morphine. For Shipman, this provided a gold mine of opportunities: he could prescribe larger doses than may have been necessary, give some to the patient and save the remaining liquid in the syringe for himself. At that time, the hospital did not keep strict records of how much pethidine was used in the different departments and because it was such a common drug, particularly in obstetrics and gynaecology, this kind of behaviour would not have seemed abnormal. What may have seemed abnormal was for a doctor, readily described by colleagues as arrogant and superior, to offer to administer the drugs himself in order to lighten the workload for nurses. For the nurses, this would have been a huge help and it would not have been in their interest to question him.

Outwardly, Shipman showed no signs of addiction and carried out his role at Pontefract to the best of his abilities – he would always be on time and well-presented and always show willing to learn more and take on extra qualifications. The only signs that were beginning to show would have been the track marks on his arms where he had been repeatedly injecting the drug into his veins. But it wouldn't be until 1975 that he was finally found out.

Shipman stayed on at Pontefract General Infirmary for a further two and a half years after completing his first year as a junior house officer. He moved through the ranks, becoming a senior house officer for two years before briefly becoming a registrar, which was followed by a swift demotion back to senior house officer. He switched frequently from medical to surgical wards and back again, eventually favouring the obstetrics and gynaecology department.

Although it cannot be proven, it is likely that Shipman started to experiment with his power and his killing potential whilst working as a junior doctor. Looking back at the paperwork, you can see that he certified a great number of deaths, more than the average house officer. Criminologists have found patterns of behavior in many serial killers around the world suggesting that they often begin to act out their fantasies in their mid- to late-twenties – which would be ten to fifteen years after the initial adolescent triggers. For Shipman, if he adhered to the profile of a serial killer, this would mean that his optimum age to start killing for real would be from around the age of twenty-seven.

Between the ages of twenty four and twenty eight, Shipman was working in Pontefract, still struggling to cope with the rigours of life as a junior doctor. He had a toddler and a baby, and his natural predisposition to superiority would have been challenged every day in the hierarchical system of medicine. In fact, on record, there is an incidence of suspected racism where Shipman regularly and openly questioned his senior supervisor, who also happened to be Asian. Looking back at Shipman's profile, it is more likely that he was simply acting out at being in a lowly position in the hospital's pecking order. He would have disliked having his work checked and his diagnoses questioned. He baulked against this one doctor to such an extent that he made him feel uncomfortable and was eventually left to do rounds on his own, or with more satellite supervision. He had bullied his way into autonomy, perhaps something he was used to in his home life, and something that became an easily transferable skill.

It was during his time in Pontefract that Shipman began to experiment further with drugs, not just on himself, but with his patients too. The first major incident recalled was that of the girl brought into the Accident & Emergency department with a bad cut on her leg. Shipman delivered a huge dose of Valium, far more than was necessary. He knew enough about opiate drugs already to be sure that she wouldn't suffer any terrible side-effects and, with only nurses around, his seniority gave him the upper hand. Perhaps at this point, he was testing the water, seeing how far he could push his power and just what he could get away with.

On the next occasion, Shipman took his experiments a step further, causing a patient to pass out after he introduced medicine too quickly into her system. He would have studied drugs and how to administer them in great detail, particularly if he was developing a morbid fascination with the subject, and so the chances are that he knew exactly what he was doing. He had a sick compulsion to witness the effects of his actions over a patient. He could control their heart-rate, respiration, levels of pain and anxiety and he got a buzz from the power.

This, in itself, is not a crime. Many doctors develop a 'God complex' and enjoy being able to have such a direct influence on their patient's health. For most, the buzz comes from helping someone to get better and to recover from illness, but for Shipman, the buzz came from his dominance and the way it put him above his patients. His own mother had instilled in him a sense of superiority and he had been playing it out his whole life, except now, the means and the rewards were much greater, and much more addictive.

Findings from the Shipman Inquiry, commissioned by the British government, strongly suggest that Shipman's first killings would have taken pace during his time in Pontefract. His reported practices indicate that he began by pushing the boundaries, seeing what effect larger and more varied doses of different drugs would have on a patient. Being stationed throughout the hospital, switching from department to department as part of his ongoing training as a house officer, patterns were unlikely to emerge and be obvious to senior members of staff. And also, because doctors in hospital are so busy, they would not have been looking out for irregular behaviour and the occasional abnormal dosage. Getting through medical school and the first year as a junior house officer bestows upon you a certain amount of trust, nobody would have dreamt that a doctor wouldn't be acting with the best interests of the patients at heart.

It is unlikely that he was able to kill during his first placement on a surgical ward; he was new and would have been monitored closely by more senior surgical staff and perhaps even some of the senior nurses. Even if he did not cause the early deaths that he would then register as part of his role, witnessing death first hand and the processes, the paperwork involved, would have sparked Shipman's interest.

Shipman rose through the ranks like any other doctor, being promoted from junior house officer to senior house officer at the end of his first year. During his first year there he had built a reputation for himself as caring and hard working, but looking back, this was more than likely a cover so that his immoral actions would not be questioned and his treatments would always be taken at face value.

Shipman preferred to work on medical wards rather than surgical – medical wards offered more freedom, less guidelines and a less structured way to treating patients. It was on the medical wards that red flags were starting to emerge. The death toll for many wards

Dr Harold Shipman on *World in Action*, ITV, 1982.

Dr Harold Shipman on *World in Action*, ITV, 1982.

Tameside Magistrates Court where Dr Harold Shipman appeared in court, charged with murdering a patient, falsifying her £300,000 will in his favour, and forging documents, 24th June 1998.

Longmead Drive, Nottingham, where Harold Shipman was brought up during his childhood.

High Pavement Grammar School, where Dr. Harold Shipman was educated, now called High Pavement College.

Harold Shipman is brought out of Stalybridge Police Station for his court appearance in Ashton, where he would face more murder charges, 12th November 1998.

Harold Shipman's son, Christopher, listens to their family solicitor (Anne Ball) deliver the statement from Mrs Shipman and family after the verdict, 31st January 1999.

Taxi Driver, John Shaw, claims to have suspected Dr Harold Shipman of murder long before the police began to investigate, 19th July 1999.

Hyde Cemetery, Greater Manchester, where many of Harold Shipman's alleged victims are buried, 24th September 1999.

IN
LOVING MEMORY
OF
KATHLEEN GRUNDY
2·7·1916 - 24·6·1998
WIFE OF JOHN
MOTHER OF ANGELA
GRANDMOTHER OF
RICHARD AND MATTHEW
DIED UNEXPECTEDLY AFTER A
LIFETIME OF HELPING OTHERS

The grave of Kathleen Grundy, one of Harold Shipman's victims. Mrs Grundy's daughter went to the police after her mother's death with regards to an altered will in favour of Harold Shipman, which subsequently sparked the investigation, uncovered a number of suspicious deaths, 24th September 1999.

Justice Forbes, the Judge in the Dr Harold Shipman murder case in Preston, 4th October 1999.

Richard Henriques QC, prosecution during the Shipman murder trial at Preston, 4th October 1999.

Primrose Shipman, Harold Shipman's wife, leaves the courtroom at Preston Crown Court, Greater Manchester on the first day of the trial, 5th October 1999.

during his working hours followed some strange and alarming patterns. Many more patients that expected would die and Shipman was present at a high percentage of the deaths, which is unusual for a busy doctor managing several wards at a time (particularly during a busy night shift). The Shipman Inquiry later suggested that he had started off using his patients as guinea pigs, seeing what effect drugs had and then realizing that when working dying and terminally ill patients, he actually had the power to end their life. An even more cynical opinion could be that he would identify the patients he thought would die in the early hours of the morning, a skill quickly learnt by hospital doctors, and instead of waiting to be called to six different cardiac arrests during the night, he would simply hasten their deaths earlier on in the evening – this making life easier for himself.

The main problem, when looking back at these early years of Shipman's career, is that all medical records have since been lost or destroyed, due to the NHS going through massive infrastructure changes, particularly during the late 1990s and early 2000s. The only way of looking back for patterns of behavior that might indicate Shipman was already killing was by looking at the death records from that time. And the death records showed some alarming statistics.

Over a six-month period in 1972, when Shipman was working on the medical wards of Pontefract General Infirmary, eighty-one deaths were registered. That in itself is not shocking, however, add to that the fact that Shipman certified seventy six of those deaths – alarm bells begin to ring. By this time in his career Shipman had a track record, if only by word of mouth, for being reckless with dosages and free and easy with pain medication. The Shipman Inquiry tentatively put forward the accusation that up to thirty-four of those deaths could have been at the hands of Shipman, either accidentally through his experiments with opiates, or more deliberately through calculated lethal doses.

Being in charge of a ward meant Shipman had direct and easy access to all patients and, as he became familiar with the staff rota and nurses' work patterns, he knew exactly when he would be alone with patients. This pattern of behavior fits with the time of deaths registered for many patients during his shifts, implying he would have been able to administer lethal injections without interruption. Unfortunately a time of death alone is not enough to pin these deaths onto Shipman and for the families of the deceased, they will never know exactly what happened in the final hours prior to their loved ones' deaths.

The large amount of deaths went unnoticed for sometime until Shipman made a mistake. A patient by the name of Phyllis Cooling had been admitted with breathing difficulties and Shipman was working as the ward doctor at that time. However, only a few hours later Phyllis had died, much to the shock of nurses on the ward and her family, who had just popped home for some supplies. Because of the lack of medical evidence, it is impossible to say whether her death came at the hands of Shipman, however, her sons remember the event well. They have spoken, on record to journalists, that they remember Dr Shipman giving her an injection. He did not tell them what the drug was, and trusting that he knew best, they did not question him either. Although there are no medical records to refer to now, there would have been at the time and several nurses, as well as a more senior doctor, such as a registrar or consultant, would have known what he had given her. The family were shocked but did not think of foul play. If colleagues had questioned the death, Shipman was able to talk his way around it – falling back on the character of himself he had built up over the years – a genial and hard-working doctor who cared deeply for his patients. If his superiors suspected Shipman was at fault, they would have been unlikely to think it was a calculated action and rather, would have assumed it was a simple mistake and that the poor doctor would be devastated. Shipman escaped any malpractice or negligence charges and nothing went on his permanent record.

If you look at this incident as a stand-alone case, then it would be crazy to link this one death to the actions of a serial killer. However, when combined with the pattern of deaths in the hospital, what we know of Shipman's MO (modus operandi) now, then it could be suggested that Cooling was one of Shipman's first victims.

Criminologists also refer to the cooling-off period following an event like this. Up until now, Shipman had been getting away with medical negligence and drug abuse. He may or may not have ended the lives of patients at the hospital and his actions and the consequences had gone unnoticed. His confidence had been building and his actions escalating. But now, he had almost been caught. He had risked losing everything through over-confidence and, like other serial killers, he went into a phase of remission. Over the next two years, only one death stands out as suspicious, compared to the thirty-four prior to this event. This near miss was a wake-up call for Shipman and it came at a canny time.

Soon after his near miss, Shipman took two weeks' leave. Most doctors in his position would have welcomed the break and taken the time to recharge their batteries, to maybe go on holiday or visit relatives. Not Shipman; he chose to spend his two weeks working as a locum in a GP practice, a practice he would later return to in order to gain vital experience in that area of medicine. Upon his return he moved to a paedeatrics ward, possibly a strategic move on his part following his near miss and rising death toll amongst his elderly patients. Making this move would force him to regain control of his killing addiction, as there was much less opportunity and many more questions would have been asked had he killed children with lethal dose of diamorphine. People readily accept that old people 'just die', but for a child to die, it is horrific and, usually, unexpected.

Shipman was welcomed into the paediatric ward with open arms and his outer demeanor helped ingratiate him with the nurses and the other doctors. He had progressed very quickly and been promoted to registrar, at least within that department. The leap from senior house officer to registrar is a big one and the title commands a great deal more respect. The initial scare from the death prior to his move may have, at first, knocked his confidence – but knowing he had, once again, got away with it and not only that, gained a promotion, meant Shipman was on a high. He had everything under control – his home life was secure thanks to the unfaltering love and support Primrose showered him with, his sick fascination with pain medication and his own addiction to pethidine had never so much as attracted a cursory raised eyebrow and now he had, more than likely, got away with murder. Had he even got away with mass murder?

As is the nature of paediatrics, very few deaths were actually registered during Shipman's time there. Investigators looking into Shipman's track record might have breathed a sigh of relief at this number, but the Shipman Inquiry later revealed that one of these deaths in particular was not as it seemed. The death of a four-year old girl, named Susie, whilst inevitable, came suddenly and as a total shock to her parents. Susie had suffered from cerebral palsy almost from birth. Cerebral palsy is a blanket term given to any number of non-specific illnesses that affect motor function and physical development; it is usually diagnosed early in life, as soon as babies are seen to not be developing in the usual way. It is thought cerebral palsy is not hereditary, but something that develops in the early stages of a child's life – from foetus the age three or four. It is a debilitating and progressive illness that affects each child differently depending on the severity. For Susie, the prognosis was not good. She was deteriorating fast and it was clear to everyone that she would die before her fifth birthday. Susie had a low quality of life, unable to move any of her limbs, talk, see or feed herself; she required round the clock care and was treated in a private room off the paediatric ward.

Shipman was in charge of treating Susie and soon after she arrived at the hospital, her condition deteriorated further – she had pneumonia, which had caused fluid to build on her lungs and she had also developed quite severe epilepsy. Shipman came across as kind and compassionate and Susie's mother recalled him speaking softly and patiently with her, explaining Susie's condition and preparing her for the worst. Shipman implied to the mother that there was little more that could be done to help Susie and that it would now just be a case of making her comfortable.

Little did she know the underlying intentions of Shipman's words; and not long after that conversation, Shipman had disappeared inside Susie's room. It is unclear whether he was alone in there, or with a nurse as well. Minutes later, Susie's mother was informed that her daughter had died. Although her death was inevitable, the suddenness of it was shocking. Susie's mother hadn't even been given the opportunity to say a final goodbye; what's more, Susie's father was not even present in the hospital, as both parents had been given the impression that her death would be a long, drawn-out affair that might last several weeks.

The Shipman Inquiry concluded that this death was most likely to have been the work of Harold Shipman, and that it was highly likely the cause of death would have been lethal injection. For some of Shipman's supporters, this incident merely confirms the compassion and mercy he showed patients, rather than the act of a psychopathic serial killer. He was 'putting her out of her misery'. Some might argue that all of Shipman's murders were really just a form of euthanasia – that he was acting out of kindness and compassion; using the powers he had for good. However, the law in the UK does not allow euthanasia, especially without the consent of the patient and their next of kin.

It is then worth considering the reason why all of Shipman's victims were seemingly near to death, either because of old age of terminal illness. Shipman had witnessed his own mother's long and drawn-out death; might she have asked him to end her life? It is common for patients dying a long and painful death to ask relatives to end their suffering. Shipman had been the favoured child; his mother placed high expectations on him and he worked tirelessly so as not to disappoint her. What if he had disappointed her with her final wish – that he end her life? Perhaps he couldn't do it, perhaps he didn't have the means, or perhaps this was never the case. But if it was, it might have triggered pathology in Shipman. Serial killers often act out past traumas in their crimes, reliving the most painful moments in their life, could it have been the same for Shipman? Putting his patients out of the misery could have been his way to combat the feelings of guilt and remorse that he couldn't help his mother in the same way. Perhaps for Shipman, every life he ended was really him trying to right a wrong, to correct what he was unable to do when he was seventeen.

After a year of paediatrics, Shipman made the curious move to obstetrics and gynaecology. For Shipman, this also came with a demotion and he fell from registrar back to senior house officer.

This was an odd move, given how popular he was in the paediatrics department and that now, should he want to become a GP (which was becoming extremely likely), he would have to do a stint in another department, because he was no longer a registrar.

So why did he move? Knowing what we know about Shipman, one might assume that he moved back to an adult medical ward because there would be more opportunities to kill. He had been starved of killing since Susie and by now his pathology must have been craving another victim. However, on the obstetrics and gynaecology ward there was also little opportunity – healthy pregnant women do not simply drop dead. Furthermore Shipman was a terrible obstetrician. Co-workers remember several patients complaining about his rough manner when examining them, one doctor even forbade Shipman to treat his wife. A friend he made on the paediatric ward, Ann Ward, told Brian Whittle of a particular time that Shipman's incompetence nearly cost the life of a young nurse, and not in his usual way – she had suffered huge internal bleeding, resulting in a haemorrhage after a routine surgical procedure carried out by Shipman.

Not being the best and being berated for his performance, as well as a distinct lack of opportunity to kill, meant there was only one reason left for Shipman's move – his addiction to pethidine. Pethidine was most commonly used and most readily available, on the obstetrics and gynaecology ward and Shipman, a user for at least four years now, would have had a habit to feed. Shipman would have been administering and prescribing the drug on a daily basis and, as previously discussed, the quantities were not strictly monitored. The easiest way for him to get his fix without detection would be by prescribing large doses to patients and then only administering a fraction – saving the rest for himself, and possibly leaving his patients in pain.

Shipman soon decided that his time at Pontefract was coming to an end. He may have felt uneasy about the death toll he was leaving behind, and having almost been caught twice (once in A&E with valium and more seriously ending the life of Susie Garfitt). His trend towards abnormally high doses of pethidine may have also been about to come under question: it was time to ship out.

He had become interested in general practice after a short placement and ensuing locum work at a local practice. The idea of being his own boss and having control over a patient's initial care would have appealed to Shipman's inflated ego. He may have also chosen to move to GP because his inadequacies as a doctor were being shown up. He was making mistakes in the obstetrics and gynaecology department, potentially due to his growing addiction, and he had been demoted back down from registrar to senior house officer.

The move to general practice would serve better Shipman's need to be 'top dog' and to have more control over his destiny. Being a GP meant he would no longer have to worry about answering to a consultant or another senior medic, because Shipman had a clear distaste for authority, possibly because he believed he was above it. Being a GP would automatically place him in the centre of a community and automatically grant him respect in society – something that he had been unable to obtain through his personality alone. It also meant he would be able to settle in with the same contacts and staff who, once manipulated into his way of thinking, would not question his prescriptions or diagnoses. There was also one major added benefit of general practice that appeals to doctors from all walks of life – free time. General practice is renowned for being slow and the job people chose if they have other priorities in life and don't want to spend an exhaustive amount of hours on hospital wards.

Not long into his stint in the obstetrics and gynaecology ward, Shipman began to look for GP positions around Yorkshire. Shipman chose the easy target of Todmorden and, having passed the exams to get into the College of General Practitioners, he answered an advert to replace a doctor due to retire. Shipman sailed through the interview and soon he and his young family were on their way to Todmorden.

Chapter 6

First Kill

First Kill

Shipman's murderous behaviour has now been dated back to the early 1970s. Some believe his first victim was Thomas Collumbine (1972), but many journalists and investigators have pinpointed Eva Lyons as Shipman's first official kill. Her drawn out death from cancer mirrored Shipman's experience with his mother. Could this have been the real trigger for his 20-year murder spree?

The fact is that we will never know who really was Shipman's first victim and any chance of finding out has gone to the grave with him. The Shipman Inquiry has pored back over thirty years of documents and medical records (where they still exist) to try and trace Shipman's movements through a trail of paperwork.

Criminologists and investigators have always sought to answer this elusive question; because to fully understand Shipman, you first need to find the catalyst, the first victim that sparked a deadly addiction to murder. To pinpoint the moment he crossed that moral line, the action that took him from only dreaming out killing to actually committing murder – that was surely the moment when everything changed.

Initially, when investigators looked into potential deaths at the hands of Shipman, they assumed that his murders would have taken place in Todmorden, where he first worked as a GP. This is a logical conclusion, given that when he was discovered, Shipman's pattern had been reoccurring in the setting of his GP practice. The next logical step would then be to look back to the start of his career as a GP and identify any unusual death certificates, of which there were many. However, it could be the case that Shipman started when he was much younger, when he was a junior doctor training at Pontefract General Infirmary, or perhaps even when he was a medical student, working in the wards of various hospitals around Leeds and South Yorkshire.

When former colleagues of Shipman were interviewed about Shipman's time in Pontefract, it became clear to all, and was later backed up by Dame Janet Smith in the Shipman Inquiry, that he had most likely murdered patients whilst working as a senior, and even junior, house officer. It has been suggested that the first killings were initially 'mercy killings', where Shipman knew the patient was nearing the end of life and simply hastened the inevitable. Was this out of pity, or was it simply his over-inflated ego thinking that he knew best when a patient should die?

A key witness from that time, Sandra Whitehead, came forward to talk about her experience on the ward, when she was a student nurse and Shipman was a young doctor. She remembers those years well, due to the high number of deaths that occurred on their wards. Not a smoking gun exactly, but Whitehead recalls that on many occasions after a death, she would find empty injection packs by the bed. During this time Shipman was present at a worryingly high number of deaths. This fact, combined with the evidence of an injection (Shipman's classic killing method) implies very strongly that Shipman was already taking lives in the early 1970s.

The Shipman Inquiry went back as far as 1971, looking at death certificates from Shipman's time on the medical wards. Some of the deaths were even noted down as 'cause for some suspicion' by the coroner. Because of the lack of complete medical records form that time, it has been hard to decide conclusively whether or not Shipman played a part in their deaths. Of the first three notable deaths, all of the 'victims' were known to be suffering from terminal illnesses, such as a brain tumour or a severe stroke; the inquiry concluded that if Shipman had caused these patients to die, it would have only brought forward the inevitable by a number of hours, not days, weeks or years as later deaths revealed. However, knowing what we know about Shipman, it seems unlikely that he would have hastened a patient's death out of kindness or compassion for their suffering. It is more likely the case that he was escalating his experiments with drugs and satisfying a growing fascination with his power over life and death.

The fourth death, that stands out in particular during those early days, is that of Edith Swift. Edith was only forty-nine and her family was not expecting her to die. Although she was Shipman's patient, there is absolutely no evidence of him prescribing or administering drugs into her system. Brian Whittle concludes that it is more than likely her death was the result of medical negligence, caused by Shipman's early experiments with the effects of drugs. And so, although these deaths are suspicious, there is no way of linking them to Shipman.

Towards the end of 1971, Shipman worked his first stint on the paediatric wards, during which time there would have been hardly any opportunity for Shipman to kill. He was still a junior doctor and nursing would have been much more hands on and intensive, so he would not have been alone with patients all that often. Plus, killing children attracts attention, something Shipman had not worked up to and was not prepared for, so he may well have curbed his cravings.

Thomas Cullumbine

Shipman moved back to the medical wards in the February of 1972. By this time Shipman would have been promoted to a senior house officer and would have had more freedom and less supervision on the wards. When the Shipman Inquiry looked into the deaths during this six-month period, they found a larger number of suspicious deaths than those noted in the previous year. Could this be a trademark pattern of escalation?

The first of these notable deaths was that of Thomas Cullumbine. There are many indicators that suggest Cullumbine was Shipman's first real victim due to similarities in his case that match traits in many of Shipman's subsequent murders. The only difference was that he was male; the majority of Shipman's victims were elderly women.

Thomas Cullumbine's records were better preserved than many other patients during that time so it is easier to see a pattern. He was admitted two months into Shipman's stint on the medical wards; he was fifty-four but in a bad way, suffering from bronchitis and emphysema. Needless to say Cullumbine was a smoker and, by all accounts, a difficult patient. Cullumbine stayed on Shipman's ward for two weeks, complaining of breathlessness and chest pains whilst simultaneously searching for cigarettes to smoke. His presence might have been beginning to grate on Shipman, who took matters into his own hands on 12th April 1972. Shipman injected Cullumbine with 10mg of morphine, which would have been a very dangerous move given the weakness of Cullumbine's lungs. Shipman would have been well aware of this and it is unknown whether he was sadistically using Cullumbine to experiment with, wanting to observe the effects of a small dose of morphine on someone with severely impaired lung function, or whether he intended to kill him with a lethal injection. Cullumbine died shortly after the injection.

It is worth noting, at this point, that many of Shipman's future victims had been described in his notes as difficult or obstructive. Cullumbine had annoyed Shipman by discharging himself and refusing to be moved to another ward. His notes from this particular case also show similarities with his notes for future victims: crossed out passages, altered doses and corrected comments all point to the work of someone covering their tracks. In fact, the notes were even amended to make it appear like morphine had never been prescribed and had been altered to the name of a different drug. The altered notes, combined with the fact that Shipman even advised his family to stay away that night points towards a premeditated murder.

Although Cullumbine was extremely ill and would have probably died within a few weeks, it is clear that his death was hastened. Could he have been Shipman's first real victim? If the others before were simply experiments gone awry, or easing the suffering of someone on death's door, then Cullumbine was different – he was murdered by Shipman.

String of Murders

If Cullumbine was the beginning of Shipman's murderous, thirty-year -long killing spree, then one death was clearly not enough. Having delved into the case of Thomas Cullumbine, the Inquiry did not have to look far to find another death, recorded by Shipman, which was shrouded in suspicion.

The very next day after Cullumbine's death, a further three deaths were recorded by Shipman. Had he ignited a fire inside his dark heart? If he did kill Cullumbine, this was the moment he had crossed the line from fantasy into reality. He had taken a life and he now he needed to take more. Was it to fill a void? Was it an addiction? Or was is just simply a case of opportunity meeting desire?

Later, when criminologists have looked back over Shipman's career, they have identified passages of time that correlate to potential 'killing sprees'. The phenomena is not unique to Shipman, in fact, it is a common trait amongst many serial killers. Between murders, the killer has time to calm down, to bask in the peaceful feelings he gets from sating his desire. This state, however, does not last for long and the urge to kill again builds inside them. Killing sprees are prime examples of serial killers continuing their pattern until the sinister intentions inside them are quelled once again.

Of the three deaths recorded the following day, the Shipman Inquiry only found one death to raise enough suspicion to link to Shipman's MO... And then another three patients died in Shipman's care just two days later. That night Shipman visited the bedsides of three elderly women. The first was Agnes Davidson, she had just had a heart attack and was recovering on Shipman's ward. The only thing to point towards her death being suspicious is that Shipman was the only attending doctor and did not call for any back up. It is unclear whether he injected her, but it seems odd, had she died of a cardiac arrest that he wouldn't have tried to resuscitate and wouldn't have called a crash team to try to save her life. Whilst Shipman was tying up the loose ends of Agnes Davidson's death, another of his patient's dropped dead, Elizabeth Thwaites. It turned out that prior to visiting Mrs Davidson, Shipman had visited Elizabeth Thwaites, alone, and administered an injection. He later noted the injection on the medical notes as Digoxin. However, the fact that he recommended not reporting her death to the coroner suggests he was covering his tracks – if he had actually injected her with morphine, the coroner would find out and his lies would be revealed. He was playing a dangerous game, riding on the assumption that his medical opinion was above question, even as a junior doctor. Had a senior consultant looked over his notes, they may well have overruled his decision to not involve the coroner and it could have all been over. The final death that night was Alice Smith – unfortunately, her medical records did not survive and the only information available came from the family, who remember that her death was unexpected and happened late at night – a pattern linked to most of Shipman's hospital killings.

The next notable suspicious death, in this cluster, was that of eighty-four year old John Brewster. Like patients he may have killed earlier, Shipman advised his family that they were not needed and could go home to collect toiletries, pyjamas etc. and bring them in the following day. But John Brewster died that night. The problem was, Shipman was getting blasé; his notes showed major inconsistencies and gaps in times, as well as downright lies. Shipman reported that Brewster had been in a coma, an unlikely outcome of a cardiac problem and also an odd situation if he was, because no other medical staff had been called during this time. Usually if a patient slips into a coma, nursing staff would be advised and the family would be called immediately – none of these things happened. Later he quoted too long a history on his notes, ranging back more than nine hours before Shipman had actually come into contact with the patient. Once again, Shipman was recorded as the only person present at his death and had ruled that it should not be reported to the coroner, even though law at that time deemed all deaths within twenty-four hours of admittance needed to be reported.

Like the cluster of women before, Brewster's passing was followed by a series of male deaths. The manner in which Thomas Ridge and John Harrison died, followed a pattern that had become apparent with the first cluster of deaths: they were treated in private rooms, late at night and only Shipman was present. Of course, this is not enough to attribute these deaths to Shipman, but the pattern does seem oddly sinister. It was followed by another two deaths, two weeks later. First Louis Bastow, whose notes were altered by Shipman, who claimed he suffered from a heart attack lasting only two minutes (previously he had written two hours and then scribbled it out). The next sudden and unexpected death was that of John Rhodes, who seemed to be in good health and was suffering from a minor illness – yet he was put in a private room. It could be conceivable that Shipman premeditated his murder, falsifying his notes to claim he was much sicker than he really was so that he would be moved to a side room where Shipman could treat him without any witnesses. The Shipman Inquiry concluded that it was highly likely that Shipman visited Rhodes secretly, as there is no record of his attendance in the notes, and murdered him via lethal injection.

This string of deaths does not actually fit the traditional profile of a serial killer. When starting out, it is unusual for serial killers to rack up a quick death toll within a couple of months. Like any addiction, they start slow, gradually picking up pace. The kills would initially be few and far between and then become more regular and higher in number. Could it be Shipman was already out of control? Could it be that this was a small number for him and that he may have killed hundreds more than the Shipman Inquiry even suggests? Or could it be that we are pinning any suspicious death in this hospital onto Shipman, because we know what he did later in life?

Unfortunately, we will never know exactly how many of these deaths were murders and how many were simply the body giving up after fighting a terrible illness. However, some things do not add up and certainly point towards foul play. For example, why was Shipman present at so many deaths? It was not his job to constantly check on patients and he should have only seen them during ward rounds. Especially since he was rarely called to a death, but usually reported one after it happened. Next is the pattern of where and when the patients were treated – all in private rooms (which could have been because they were seriously ill anyway) and all at night (which could have been because there were less staff available to help resuscitate). The altered notes also point towards secret and questionable behavior, especially knowing how Shipman falsified the records of later victims. However, none of this evidence is concrete enough to say 100% whether he killed them. The Shipman Inquiry certainly suggests that he had a hand in many of their deaths.

Susie Garfitt

Shipman moved back to the paediatrics ward, but this time as a registrar. Being a registrar gave him even more power and control over his work life and it was much easier for him to command the respect of nursing staff and other doctors. His move came after a spree of possible killings had left a staggering death toll and a few unanswered questions. In fact, he almost tripped himself up with the death (or murder) or Phyllis Cooling, after he had administered a mysterious injection and narrowly escaped a malpractice lawsuit.

The move to paedeatrics offered less opportunity to kill, but there still was at least one death that came under scrutiny. The death of a four-year old girl, named Susie Garfitt, came suddenly and as a total shock to her parents. Susie had been suffering from cerebral palsy almost from birth and her death was somewhat inevitable. Cerebral palsy is a non-specific illness that affects the brain – debilitating motor function and physical development; it is usually diagnosed early in life, as soon as babies are seen to not be developing in the usual way.

Susie was deteriorating fast. She had a poor quality of life; she was unable to move any of her limbs, talk, see or feed herself. This meant that she required round the clock care and was treated in a private room off the paediatric ward.

For Shipman, Susie may have provided the perfect opportunity to calm his cravings to kill. In paedeatrics he would have come across far fewer dying patients and the death of a child would have been far harder for staff, relatives and the coroner to accept. It is also worth noting that, during his time in paedeatrics, Shipman's addiction to pethidine became worse. Perhaps he was self-medicating in order to numb himself from his own murderous urges.

Shipman was in charge of treating Susie and soon after she arrived at the hospital, her condition deteriorated further – she had pneumonia, which had caused fluid to build on her lungs and she had also developed quite severe epilepsy. Shipman would have come across as soft and reassuring, keeping up the façade of a caring doctor meant it was less likely for people to think he was acting inappropriately. Shipman implied to the mother that there was little more that could be done to help Susie and also implied that she could relax, get a cup of tea, that her death was not imminent.

This implication, which he used with many friends and relatives, meant that he had time alone and uninterrupted with his patient. Many families who have come forward about their loved ones' deaths have reported Shipman implying they could take some time for themselves, or go and collect some overnight belongings. No one has reported Shipman actually bothering to call relatives to warn them that the time was near and that they should hurry to the hospital.

It is unknown whether he was alone in with Susie, or whether he was with a nurse as well. Given the nature of Susie's condition and his seniority as a registrar, it could have been the case that he manipulated a nurse into his way of thinking and that she was complicit in Susie's death. Not long after he had been alone with Susie, a nurse informed Susie's mother that she had passed away. Neither Susie's mother, nor her father (who wasn't even at the hospital at the time) were given the opportunity to say goodbye, which surely would have been the case had staff known she was about to die.

The Shipman Inquiry concluded that this death was most likely to have been the work of Harold Shipman. It's true that Susie was terminally ill and close to death, but the suddenness and speed of her actual death does not fit with the usual type of death experienced by

someone suffering from cerebral palsy. The Inquiry stated that
it was highly likely that the cause of Susie's death would have been
lethal injection.

Ruth Highley – Todmorden

The rest of Shipman's time at Pontefract went by without suspicion,
perhaps because of his growing addiction to pethidine and perhaps
because working in paedeatrics and obstetrics and gynaecology
offered little chance to kill.

Shipman joined the Abraham Ormerod Medical Centre in
Todmorden as an assistant principal GP on March 1st 1974. Some
people, particularly the residents of Todmorden, believe that his first
killing took place just two months into his time at the practice. On
May 10th, he signed the first death certificate of his career as a GP
and it was for the seventy-two year old Ruth Highley. She had died,
according to Shipman, of kidney failure.

There is little evidence to link Shipman to her death because Mrs
Highley was cremated and the medical records from that time were
destroyed long ago. In Todmorden, a deep suspicion about her death
remains; it could well be that Mrs Highley was Shipman's first victim,
if we assume the deaths in the hospital were simply acts of
negligence rather than premeditated murder. Looking at the deaths
that Shipman has actually been convicted of murder for, Mrs Highley
does fit the pattern. However, there is insufficient evidence to prove
this theory.

It wasn't until early in 1975 that Shipman's records first show signs
of following the same killing pattern for which he was convicted, and
so perhaps it is here that we should look for his first official kill?

Shipman's killing in the 1990s, the killings he was convicted of, all happened in the same way. He would be visited by a patient and would then arrange for a house visit. Once he was in the house he would administer a lethal dose of diamorphine, either waiting for death and then pronouncing it with the family present, or more usually leaving and letting the body be discovered by friends or relatives. Because his victims were old and usually suffering from some kind of illness, most of the time the death was accepted as a natural end.

His first victim to die this way was Elizabeth Pearce. She was eighty-four and lived with her daughter. Elizabeth was suffering from the usual afflictions of old age and was very frail. She had visited the surgery complaining of shortness of breath and then was found dead the following day.

Although Elizabeth's death is the first to fit Shipman's pattern – there is unfortunately no proof that he was ever in her house just prior to, or during, her death.

Eva Lyons

Shipman continued to maintain a suspiciously high level of attendance at the death of his patients. Something very odd for a GP, particularly when many died at home. Although it was common, particularly in the 1970s and 1980s for doctors to visit their patients, surely those that were close to death would have been sent to hospital by their caring and concerned GP? Professor Richard Baker, from the University of Leicester, as part of his Government-commissioned brief to examine the Shipman murders, suggested Shipman was present at an abnormal and alarming amount of his patients' deaths. In about 40% of cases, Shipman was with his patient when they died, which is shocking when compared to the national average of 0.8%.

The next notable death was that of Eva Lyons and it would have touched a raw nerve with Shipman as her illness, and subsequent deterioration from throat cancer, would have reminded him of his own mother's tragic death.

Many journalists and investigators have pinpointed Eva Lyons as Shipman's first official victim since leaving Pontefract General Infirmary. Some believe the deaths at Pontefract to be attributed to negligence and not premeditation, and even go so far as to call Eva Lyons Shipman's first official kill.

Eva Lyons was suffering a long and drawn out death. Shipman took on her case and attended to her regularly between her hospital stays. He would call in almost every other day, forming an unhealthy attachment to the dying woman. Shipman, like the doctor who visited his mother, would administer painkillers through an intravenous line. It would have been impossible for him not to draw comparisons between Eva and his own mother. Her husband and family reported that whilst she was in pain, she was still upbeat and chatty and still functioning in life.

On the night of her death, Shipman visited the family late, perhaps hoping to catch Mrs Lyons alone. Her administered her pain medication at 11pm in the presence of her husband and then casually announced her death just twenty minutes later. He made no attempt to resuscitate or call an ambulance.

The Shipman Inquiry concluded that Shipman administered a lethal overdose of morphine to speed up the death of Eva Lyons. Whilst it was likely Mrs Lyons was in a lot of pain, it was still not Shipman's decision to make. Perhaps she and her husband had wished for a peaceful end to her life. Either way, Shipman broke the law and ended her life prematurely.

Marie West

Poring over past documents and analysing Shipman's behaviour undoubtedly shines the light on hundreds of patients who later turned out to be victims of Shipman's lethal injections. The Shipman Inquiry identified a pattern of behaviour and a string of suspicious deaths that must have been the work of Shipman. However, Shipman was only ever convicted of fifteen murders, which still made him Britain's most prolific serial killer.

The first of Shipman's victims, for whose death he was actually convicted, was Marie West. The eighty-one year old was murdered on March 6th 1995 and like his other victims, she died in her home. Shipman had gained the trust of Marie West, who had followed him to his new surgery. Her friend, Marion Hadfield, also placed her trust in Shipman, because she was even in the house during the murder.

Shipman administered a lethal injection of diamorphine into Mrs West's system, whilst her friend waited politely in the kitchen. Not longer after, Shipman announced that she had died of a massive stroke. By this point he had gained so much respect and unquestioning trust from his local community that no one questioned why he never called an ambulance, or never even called in Marie's friend so that she was with someone in her dying moments.

Marie West's medical records were found in Shipman's home following a police raid, along with hundreds of others. Could it be that Shipman kept deceased victim's records as trophies of his kills?

Whilst it is clear to all that Marie West was not Shipman's first victim, she is the earliest victim whose murder he was later found guilty of.

Elaine Oswald

So now we have established a few key victims who have the potential to be Shipman's first. But there is one interesting case – a person who could be the sole survivor of Shipman's needle.

Elaine Oswald, at the age of 25, would have been an anomaly in Shipman's MO and so it is more likely that he was just experimenting with drugs and their effect. She came to his surgery suffering from a mild stomach ache. 'It was just so cool having a young attractive doctor there,' she told the Telegraph newspaper. 'He had very pale blue eyes and looked like the doctors on television.'

Shipman told Mrs Oswald that he needed to take some blood samples. He then prescribed Diconal, a type of morphine, and suggested she leave her front door open so he could let himself in. Diconal would have been a drastic measure to take for a simple stomach ache and hints at Shipman's disregard for opiate misuse.

Upon her return, Oswald dutifully left her front door open so that Shipman could just walk in. His position as a community GP had endeared him to the community so much that this did not seem like an abnormal request and was a scenario that would repeat itself again and again over the next twenty years.

Mrs Oswald's last memory before losing consciousness was of seeing Dr Shipman approach her with a hypodermic needle in his hand. 'The next thing I know, I'm lying on the floor. There are a lot of people in my bedroom. My mouth's bleeding, there's blood trickling down my mouth. I can't breathe, my ribs are hurting every time I try. The people in the room are shaking me, slapping my face. All I wanted to do was sleep, just sleep for ever.' She told the Telegraph journalist of her ordeal.

Shipman later claimed she must have suffered a severe allergic reaction to the pain medication, evading any insinuation that he might have administered the wrong dosage. He had made a mistake. Either he had pushed an opiate experiment too far, or he had failed to kill his patient. He made up for it by visiting her in hospital almost every day, and later insisted on inviting her and her husband to dinner. Perhaps he genuinely felt guilty, or more than likely, he was trying to keep up his reputation as a trusted and highly regarded community physician. For years, Oswald thought he was her saviour and only after reading newspaper reports of Shipman's MO and his terrible list of victims did Mrs Oswald, now living in America, suspect he had tried to kill her.

The truth is, we will never know for sure who Shipman's first victim really was. According to the letter of the law, Marie West was his first kill, because she is the earliest victim whose murder has been assigned to Shipman. Going back further through his time as a GP, both in Todmorden and Hyde, any number of suspicious deaths could have been the work of Harold Shipman. The two most likely being either Eva Lyons, who is often given the unwelcome title as Shipman's first victim or Ruth Highley, the first person to die under Shipman's care as a GP. Eva Lyons certainly fits the MO that Shipman later continued to use; furthermore, her death echoes that of his late mother suggesting she could have been the spark that ignited the fire of hundreds more murders. Having not been able to help his mother in her suffering, perhaps he saw the similarities and, somewhere in his twisted mind, believed he was honouring his late mother's memory by putting a poor woman, suffering from the same terminal illness, out of her misery. As previously discussed, Shipman's childhood was shaped by constant efforts to please his mother; not helping her die could have been the final disappointment that he couldn't make amends for. Prematurely ending the life of Eva Lyons may have been his way of atoning for letting down his own mother on her deathbed when he was powerless to help.

Going back further than his GP days, the Shipman Inquiry revealed a large number of suspicious deaths where Shipman was present, or had recorded the death. The deaths do not follow his later MO and the only evidence to support claims that he was responsible comes from analysing patterns and drawing conclusions from death certificates. Although we will never be able to pin these deaths to Shipman 100%, it does seem likely that he killed a number of patients during his time in Pontefract. The deaths could have been mercy killings, which is still inexcusable and purely highlights Shipman's arrogance for believing he knew best when a person should die. Or the deaths could simply have been a case of medical negligence; during that time Shipman had a strong addiction to pethidine and was a junior doctor with ideas above his station. The deaths could have been a result of simple dosage and diagnosis mistakes, or more disturbingly, they could have been a result of botched secret experiments that Shipman carried out because of his sinister obsession with drugs and their effect.

Shipman's first victim remains a matter of opinion and a secret that went to the grave with him when he chose to take his own life.

Chapter 7

Todmorden

Todmorden

Todmorden is a town that got a lucky escape. Shipman worked there for just eighteen months, between 1974 and 1975. The inhabitants of Todmorden could have suffered a very different fate, but Shipman was fined for forging prescriptions for Pethidine, and attended a drug rehabilitation clinic in York. He then set up a clinic in Greater Manchester. During his short time in Todmorden, it is thought that he was responsible for at least seven deaths.

Todmorden is a quiet town in the Peak District. It is pretty remote and lies almost smack bang between Manchester and Leeds. It is technically in Yorkshire, but is actually only about twenty miles from Manchester and has more affiliation with Lancashire than Yorkshire. It is rural and picturesque and an unlikely choice for a young doctor, who one would assume might prefer to locate to a more lively and busy city.

Shipman moved to Todmorden in March 1974, where he joined the busy staff at Abraham Ormerod Medical Centre. The surgery was suffering from a staffing crisis and had needed a GP to join the staff pretty urgently. The job advertised was for an assistant senior GP and he answered and interviewed for the position whilst working in obstetrics and gynaecology at Pontefract General Infirmary.

The other members of staff would have been relieved to have him on board. The practice was one of only two surgeries in the town and, despite its rural location, the population was pretty large.

Three full-time doctors were looking after nearly 12,000 patients and so Shipman was welcomed with open arms. He would replace a senior GP who had retired due to ill health. The patients of the practice were used to a certain type of doctor, due to the close-knit community environment and luckily, Shipman's outer demeanour of being helpful and always going the extra mile placed him in good favour amongst town folk and colleagues alike.

Dr Michael Grieve was one of the other doctors working at the surgery in Todmorden and has been a key character witness for investigators looking back at Shipman's short time in Todmorden. Dr Grieve remembers how he impressed at interview stage both with knowledge and attitude. Shipman certainly made an impression on the old stalwarts at Abraham Omerod Medical Centre. He was the youngest doctor by far, and instead of feeling young and inexperienced because this was his first time working as a GP, he instead immediately began to suggest improvements and ideas for modernisations. At the time, his enthusiasm was looked upon favourably and his knowledge of new protocols and systems were called upon to help modernise the practice. In hindsight, this may have just been another display of Shipman's arrogance, or him thinking he knew best all the time. It would take a confident person to walk into an established practice with no experience and start recommending changes.

Shipman not only made suggestions for improvements, he also took on the challenge for himself. He in fact offered to take hundreds of patient records and files home with him to 'cut down' the medical notes so that only the vital information was there. He claimed this was to prepare for the eventual digitalisation of medical records, but a cynical person may think there were ulterior motives behind this supposed act of generosity. What young doctor with a wife and two children would want to spend his free time trolling through medical records and cutting them down, just in case, they needed to be typed on to a computer in the future? Perhaps this was actually a premeditated act that would allow him to see all the patients' files, making it easy to pick out victims and allowing him to see what standard was required of his own notes – to see what scribbles would go by unnoticed.

Shipman's apparent eagerness to please went down well with his colleagues. Dr Grieve also recalled how many patients on their list were housebound; housebound patients required regular GP visits and on their rounds it was common for the GPs to also stop by at other patients' houses along the way. For most young doctors coming out of a hospital environment, this would have seemed terribly old-fashioned and irksome, not to mention time consuming. However, this old-school way of doctoring suited Shipman to a tee. It meant he was able to build up trust and rapport with his patients, a trust he could later abuse. Shipman was also hands-on when it came to injections and taking blood; unlike other doctors who would pass the work on to nurses or phlebotomists, Shipman always liked to do it himself. The patients loved the extra attention they received, but for Shipman it was probably just another form of control and a way to ingratiate himself amongst the community. The more genial and caring he came across, the less people would suspect him of malpractice and murder.

His charm offensive worked and he was soon offered a full-time position at the surgery. The news of a permanent position as a GP meant an impressive pay rise and for the first time he was able to purchase a house for his family to live in. The Shipmans moved to a popular area of Todmorden known as Sunnyside – so called because it was situated on the side of a valley that got the most sun. The Shipmans bought a Victorian style terrace and named it Sunnybank. Neighbours who have been interviewed after Shipman's arrest remembered the Shipmans as a pleasant enough family. Primrose quickly developed a reputation for being a little snobby as well as brash and unkempt. She had obviously changed since the days of inviting Harold's medical student friends around for tea and cake. By 1974, she had being bringing up two children almost single-handedly (due to the long hours Shipman spent in the hospital). She had gained weight and was unable to keep a tidy house and clean children. Interestingly though, neighbours recall her children playing in the street and socialising with others – the complete opposite of both Harold's and Primrose's upbringings.

Fred quickly became well-known and well-liked in the community. He would be the go-to person if you were ill, or needed a doctor for a house visit. Many said he had a good sense of humour and really seemed to care for his patients. He provided the best of both worlds for the community of Todmorden – knowledge of modern systems and practice combined with a more old-fashioned approach to patient care. Shipman even became involved with the local community. He attended meetings and joined the Rochdale Canal Society – a club set up to help revive the waterways, weirs and locks that had fallen into disrepair.

It may have seemed that Shipman was just a nice, down-to-earth doctor who liked to be involved in his local community. But his motives were more sinister and disturbing. For Shipman, it was always about being the best, and that extended to every aspect of his life. He had to be the best GP, the best carer, the best at paperwork, the best at canal restoration, etc. He needed to be loved and trusted because without that, his ego would be bruised. Shipman's ego was the key to everything and his every action was to bolster his own inflated ego.

But Shipman was hiding another secret, besides his urges to kill – he had a drug problem. Throughout his years in Pontefract, Shipman's abuse of the drug pethidine had increased. He managed the addiction well, never showing outward signs of abuse. His poor performance as an obstetrician in his last placement, and the shocking number of deaths in his care had gone unnoticed, so drug-abuse was never suspected. He would have developed established channels for obtaining the drug, channels that had been tried and tested as above question. So it is likely that coming to Todmorden, Shipman would have been confident that he could, once again, obtain pethidine for personal use and that no one would be any the wiser.

As a GP, Shipman had even more freedom than before. He had a drugs book and a drugs bag allowing him to keep stores of various substances in case he needed them on an urgent house call. He was also able to collect prescriptions on behalf of his patients, which meant he could write a prescription for pethidine, collect it and then keep it, and his patient would never know it was even on their record. It was also common practice to order pethidine on behalf of midwives, and because everything was logged using pen and paper, it would have been easy for Shipman to fudge the numbers, keeping some back for himself.

It might have seemed like he'd landed on a gold mine of pethidine, but it was a double-edged sword. Now Shipman had access to as much pethidine as he liked, his usage increased and his prescriptions and orders for the drug were attracting attention.

In 1975, there was an inquiry into Shipman's pethidine orders. It seems the surgery had been ordering a substantially increased amount of the drug since Shipman had started working there and his name was on most of the orders. His arrogance was getting the better of him once again. He had thought that he could just get away with anything, no doubt because he had for so long. But the time and effort he had put in making people believe that he was a wonderful person paid off. Both the Home Office and the West Yorkshire Police got in contact with the pharmacies that supplied the surgery. The pharmacists all said the same thing, that Shipman was competent and efficient – there was no way he was an addict, he certainly did not come across that way. Carole Peters quoted the police report from the time, "It would seem that there is no drug abuse by Dr Shipman. A watch will be maintained and should anything further come to light then a further report will be submitted." In total, Shipman would acquire over 30,000mg of pethidine just by writing out prescription for 'practice use' and there may have been more that he obtained by using his patients' prescriptions.

Shipman continued to work in his practice unaware that the Home Office were monitoring his pethidine orders. And a number of suspicious deaths started to be registered. The first death happened only two weeks into Shipman working at the practice. Maria Highley was the first of Shipman's patients to die when he was in the role of GP. Investigations into her death have been inconclusive, but his presence there meant one of two things: either he was responsible, or the experience had planted a seed.

There were several suspicious deaths during Shipman's time in Todmorden and one very tragic incident. The young doctor had become all too familiar with the drug pethidine and its effects, but he still managed to misjudge it. He administered a large dose of the drug to a mother during childbirth. Unfortunately, the drug passed through her system, through the placenta and into the baby's bloodstream. The baby boy, named Christian, was delivered but with breathing complications and the next day Shipman was called back to the house where he panicked and tried to revive the child on his own, instead of calling for an ambulance. The child died and Shipman was said to be devastated. Killing healthy children was not part of his MO, and the way this death affected him highlights how unmoved he was by every other death he encountered. He would have known that the death was his fault and a consequence of his negligence, but, yet again, he got away with it. The coroner did not do a toxicology test and instead out the death down to 'sudden infant death syndrome'.

This incident was soon followed by the botched experiment-attempted murder of Elaine Oswald. Shipman's only known survivor, Oswald, witnessed first hand him injecting her. However, he didn't inject her with a lethal dose and, instead, tried to revive her and call for help. It may well have been the case that Shipman's pethidine usage was starting to cloud his judgement. He had made a mistake with baby Christian and perhaps he saw an opportunity to experiment and perfect what was the correct dosage for a young woman. His body would have become so resilient to the drug that what seemed like a small amount to him, could have been lethal to someone else. Perhaps Elaine Oswald's brush with death was simply a confused Shipman trying to regain control of a drug that was beginning to take control of him.

By the following year, Shipman was settled at the practice in Todmorden and it is at this time that victims fitting Shipman's MO began to fall. Eva Lyons is generally regarded as Shipman's first

official victim, but there were three more potential victims
before that.

Elizabeth Pearce was old and frail and died at home. It is thought
by the community of Todmorden that Shipman was responsible for
her death, however no one knows for sure if he visited her and
administered one of his lethal injections. However, the next two
people to die were most definitely visited by Shipman. Bob Lingard
was suffering from breathing problems and was known to the surgery
as someone who was close to death. Shipman visited his home and
was present when he died. As soon as Lingard had died, Shipman was
onto the next. He visited Lily Crossley and gave her an injection of
some kind, not informing her relatives what he was administering her.
Lily died an hour later. Whilst few witness statements and records of
these incidents remain, it seems highly suspicious that two people
died on the same night, having both been visited and medicated by
Dr Shipman. The fact that no one in the village questioned this
shows what an amazing job Shipman had done at immersing himself
in the community and making them feel like he was one of them, an
ally and a friend.

Eva Lyons was the most notable victim of this period, perhaps due
to the nature of her death and the similarities she shared with
Shipman's mother. She was dying from throat cancer and records and
witness statements from her husband and daughter all suggest that
Shipman hastened her death with a lethal injection, either of
pethidine, or diamorphine. She is the first of his victims where there
is solid evidence of his MO. The death was unremarkable and slipped
through the coroner's net. He had gotten away with murder and this
simple, but effective, way of killing would be how Shipman would
proceed in the future.

But he nearly lost that opportunity just as he was getting started. What nobody had realized was that his pethidine abuse was getting out of hand. The Home Office's initial investigation had caused one concerned pharmacist to look over Shipman's orders of the drug. The amount was abnormally large and she raised her concerns with another doctor at the surgery, Dr John Dacre. Dr Dacre decided to run his own secret investigation, looking into all of the patients who had been prescribed pethidine. He then went to visit each patient and, unsurprisingly, found that none of them had any recollection of being prescribed the drug, nor of receiving it.

Dr Dacre and his colleagues staged an intervention, confronting Shipman at the end of a shift. Shipman appeared humble and admitted he did use the drug recreationally – although he did not let on as to the extent. The doctors also recalled moments that, looking back, would have been obvious that he was abusing drugs. Shipman often suffered from blackouts and seizures and doctors, as well as patients, at the surgery had witnessed these on more than one occasion. In fact, on one memorable night, Shipman actually collapsed in his home. He had either taken too much pethidine and knocked himself unconscious, or suffered a seizure from the withdrawal effects. Primrose did not know what to do; so she called his colleagues at the surgery, who rushed over to check on him. They immediately called an ambulance. But Shipman was even prepared for this – he used his medical knowledge to explain away symptoms and narrowly avoid a full examination. If he had been examined, doctors would have realized the extent of his addiction. He had been injecting all over his body for years and many of his veins had collapsed and entry wounds had become infected.

Shipman initially agreed to seek help and admit himself into hospital to deal with the problem. But he later became abusive and obstructive and they had no choice but to threaten him with dismissal. Shipman was angry and stormed out of the surgery. For him, it was imperative to regain control of the situation, because Shipman was a control freak. He could not have others controlling his fate in this way, so he took matters into his own hands. Knowing a dismissal would not stand him in good stead for the future, he resigned in a rage – throwing his doctor's bag at the surgery door. Primrose, the ever-dutiful wife, was caught up in the whirlwind. She and her children were told that they were going to have to leave the following day. Shipman admitted himself into Halifax General Infirmary, knowing this was the smart thing to do in order to appear humble, whilst his wife was left to fend for herself and had no choice but to return to her parents in Wetherby.

Shipman was treated by a psychiatrist and was then referred to a rehab clinic, known as 'The Retreat'. Shipman went through cold turkey withdrawals and spent more time recovering at the rehabilitation centre.

At the clinic he was visited by police and questioned about his drug usage and how he obtained such large quantities of pethidine. Shipman refused to answer their questions at first, a tactic he would later employ when questioned about his murder victims. Shipman lied and changed his story several times, claiming he only took the drug from time to time because he was depressed – unhappy that his colleagues ostracized him both at work and socially. This, of course, was not true and the efforts Shipman had made to integrate himself within the community contradicted this explanation.

The police could not be sure about the extent and severity of his abuse, but they still charged him with obtaining a controlled substance through deception, unlawful possession of a controlled substance, as well as forging prescriptions.

His arrest rocked the Shipmans' world. He was forced to sell his home and his stake in the GP practice. He had to sign a declaration that stated he 'had no intention to return to general practice'. Despite his deception and negligent behavior, Shipman still managed to attract support from the people of Todmorden, who always seemed to think the best of him and felt sorry that life and work had become so hard that he had to turn to drugs. Some even appeared in court as character witnesses in his defence.

Shipman was given a relatively small fine compared to what he would have earned as a doctor and, remarkably, he was not struck off and no restrictions were placed on his medical license. Shipman obviously did a good job of convincing the court that his addiction was not as bad as it actually was, that it hadn't gone on for that long and that, really, he was the victim of a stressful work situation that drove him to drugs because the system had failed to support him. By now, he was used to getting away lightly, but this would have been a major victory and a massive boost to his ego.

Unfortunately, Primrose's family did not have such a sympathetic view. Edna Oxtoby, Primrose's mother, already disapproved of Shipman, and this simply added fuel to the fire. In the months after the court case, the Shipmans were forced to leave Todmorden and the Oxtobys provided a home for Harold, Primrose and their two children. But as soon as they had found their feet, Primrose ceased all contact with her family. No one knows why for sure; it may have been that she had grown tired of her overbearing mother and her constant disapproval, or it was more likely that Shipman could not cope with someone not liking him – he had always been the best and the favoured one, it would have been a constant knock to his ego, knowing there was one person who saw him for who he really was.

The Shipmans briefly moved to Durham, where Harold secured a job as a clinical medical officer. Here he took stock and laid low, knowing people would want to see a rehabilitated man. But he had a craving he needed to satisfy and his current job did not allow any perks, such as free access to controlled substances like morphine. It wasn't long before Shipman was applying for his second job as a GP.

Chapter 8

Hyde

Hyde

Shipman spent most of his life in Hyde and this is where the majority of his murders took place. He worked hard to ingratiate himself with the local community, gaining their trust before he let himself into their homes and killed them. Even today, there are still people in Hyde who believe that Shipman was innocent and the victim of a witch-hunt instigated by former colleagues at the Donneybrook Medical Centre.

It had only been three years since Shipman had passed the exams required to become as GP, known at the MRCGP (Member of the Royal College of General Practitioners). Since then he had only worked for nineteen months in an actual role as a GP. This may have continued for many years in Todmorden had he not been found out as a drug addict. Perhaps the people of Todmorden got a lucky escape, because even in those short nineteen months, Shipman had probably killed at least four of his patients and ruined the lives of others through malpractice.

After a brief spell in Durham, working in a desk job, he returned to general practice (not mentioning that he had signed a statement in court saying he had no intention to work in general practice again). Shipman arrived at the Donneybrook practice in Hyde on 1st October 1977 at the age of thirty-one. He joined a team of six other doctors, who had come together to form the practice ten years earlier. The Donneybrook practice was new and modern (for its time) and had been especially created by two doctors from separate practices who teamed up together.

It's hard to believe a former drug addict, who was forced to leave his previous role and admit himself into rehab, would have been a successful candidate. But Shipman was obviously a charmer. He openly admitted to his pethidine usage (although not the extent), and gave them his psychiatrist's details. On the surface he appeared genuine and honest from the start, but he failed to mention one thing – he wasn't supposed to be working in general practice ever again. Being open and up-front was a good decision; it endeared him to his future colleagues and also gained their trust immediately. Not one of them delved any further into his drug abuse or criminal conviction.

Working as a GP is like being self-employed. The seven GPs at Donneybrook had a co-operative system where they each earned money depending on their workload and patient list. GPs earn money through hospital referrals, administering jabs and for extra services, such as taking blood and other medical tests. Shipman endeared himself to the community once again. He was remembered as amiable and competent and always had time for his patients. He would often take their calls directly and made the largest number of house calls. News soon spread of this new doctor and people queued up to join his list; soon he had 2,300 patients. Shipman was different to other doctors in that he seemed to go the extra mile for his patients – he would make house calls just to check if everything was all right rather than advising them to come back if the problem persists. This made for long working hours and he was always in the surgery early and usually finished late, leaving Primrose at home on her own.

Home for the Shipmans was initially a rented property whilst he was on trial, and then after his six-month probation period was up, they bought a house in Roe Cross Green, which is where Shipman lived until his arrest. Although he was a doctor, Shipman was not in a good way financially – he had a large loan he had to take out in order to buy into the Donneybrook practice (a common occurrence for GPs), he also had court fines to pay and the hangover of not being able to work whilst in rehab and recovery. So the house was shabbier and less impressive than a house you might expect a high-flying doctor to own.

Although Shipman fit in well within the community and with his fellow doctors, his true colours began to show when he spoke to the receptionists at the surgery. He would usually talk down to them and belittle them for the slightest mistake or inaccuracy. His main target was Vivien Langfield, who managed the auxiliary staff in the practice. Shipman most likely took issue with her because she stood up for her staff. Shipman was used to being in control and never being questioned. On many an occasion Shipman would insist she give people the sack, usually for no good reason. Shipman had a superior attitude toward the non-doctors and regularly berated them in front of colleagues and patients. Those who did talk back or stand up to Shipman became targets and it wasn't long before he'd find a reason to fire them. Shipman was very good at throwing his weight around. Vivien and other administration staff have since described him as a bully. Although he was more polite with the doctors, he still forced through his own ideas and opinions.

Many of the women wondered how he must treat his own wife, given the way he spoke to them. From the outside, Primrose and Harold seemed happy in their new life and they soon put down roots and began to extend their family. They had two more children – David, who was born on 20th March 1979 and Sam, who was born on 5th April 1982.

In the early years, Shipman fully immersed himself in the community, joining parent-teacher groups and volunteering on medical councils. He even became a mentor for a young doctor with a drug problem. To his patients, he seemed like the perfect doctor, he would make regular house calls, many of which were unscheduled. This may seem odd now, but in the late 1970s and early 1980s this would have been fairly normal and certainly something the older generation were used to. Doctors during this time gained heavier and heavier workloads, but this did not deter Shipman and he continued to keep an eye on his most vulnerable and elderly patients. From the outside, this would have come across as caring and compassionate and explains why people were desperate to get on his patient list. However, it is clear now that he had ulterior motives and wanted to gain the trust of old and vulnerable women living on their own.

In other areas, however, his unpleasant side was beginning to seep through the cracks. He became known for his bad temper around the office and staff knew when to keep their heads down and not make a fuss. By his early thirties, Shipman had developed a real skill for berating others, more than likely to feed his egomania, and he was particularly good at picking out targets. On more than one occasion, ex-colleagues remember him tearing apart a young drugs rep so much that she was reduced to tears. He would prove his own self-importance by humiliating others and openly calling them up on their mistakes, and if anyone were to challenge him they would pay the price – usually with their job. He kept himself to himself and rarely socialized with his work colleagues; he hardly ever joined them for lunch, which was generally taken in the reception area, instead he was out visiting patients. People just assumed he was a workaholic and because he was well-loved by his patients and seemed to be performing well in his job, nobody ever questioned him. Something he was now used to and expected in every situation in life.

Shipman's father died in 1985 and his reaction to the death was a little disturbing to those around him. He showed no emotion whatsoever. The same doctor who had been traumatized at the death of a baby he had delivered could barely show the slightest sign of emotion at his father's death. He did not have a particularly close relationship with his father, but there is nothing to suggest that he disliked him or was estranged from him. Shipman had barely been in touch with his family and his indifference angered his siblings, Pauline and Clive.

Shipman also became disparaging about his patients. It was clear he liked to visit their homes on his terms (perhaps another sign of his controlling nature), and he would get annoyed when they returned to the surgery regularly. He would make sarcastic comments about them and moan that they were clogging up the waiting room. Just like one of his first victims, Thomas Cullumbine, it could have been the case that Shipman later targeted these 'problem patients' in order to bring order to his work life. It is worth considering that Shipman was such a control freak that dying people and the elderly just made his patient list untidy and he would rather take control and eradicate them rather than wait for them to die.

Indeed, many suspicious deaths took place during his time at Donneybrook, the Shipman Inquiry later revealed that his pattern escalated, starting with between two and four people a year until the early 1980s. At this point the killings escalated to between nine and twelve unnecessary deaths a year.

Most of Shipman's victims were old women, and whilst it is thought that he had some kind of pathological preference towards women, his early killings in Pontefract dispute this and it is more likely the case that they were easy targets. A lot of Shipman's patients were widows who had heard good things about his thorough care and old-fashioned methods, which involved more house visits and less time in the surgery – this was a bonus for them. The fact that they were old also meant that the deaths were more likely to go unnoticed as death in old age in usually expected and accepted more readily.

Some of the deaths investigated by the Shipman Inquiry found insufficient evidence to attribute them to Shipman and so the first real case to consider is that of eighty-six year old Sarah Marsland. Marsland was paid an unannounced visit by Shipman in August 1978; she lived alone and during his visit, Shipman claimed her death was due to a coronary embolism. Strangely, he was in attendance at the death of Mary Jordan later that month and gave the exact same reason for her death. It must have seemed very odd that he was present at both deaths and that both women died of the same thing. But who would check? The process of certifying a death is left in the hands of the GP. If the GP decides that there is no need to refer the death to a coroner, then his word is taken at face value. Furthermore, it is unlikely the two families would talk to each other about the intricacies of their late relatives' deaths and his colleagues would have been far too busy with their own workloads to worry about two old ladies that had died of a condition common in the elderly.

That winter, Shipman embarked on another killing spree, this time with cancer patients. Echoing the treatment he witnessed his mother receive all those years ago, Shipman would visit his patients' houses and administer pain relief in the form of diamorphine. Treating cancer patients gave Shipman unique access to diamorphine. He could prescribe large doses, claiming the patients were in terrible pain, and keep some back for future kills.

True to his MO, Shipman visited his patients at home and administered a lethal dose of diamorphine. In this fashion, he prematurely took the life of Harold Bramwell on 7th December, as well as two non-confirmed cases on 25th September and the 5th of December. Once his cancer patients had died, he would have been able to take their excess pain medication and keep it for himself. If questioned by the family, he would have told them that he was taking it away to be disposed of, as only medical professionals are allowed to be in charge of controlled substances.

It is likely that Shipman then used his saved up diamorphine to end the life of Annie Campbell on 20th December 1978. Unimaginatively, he also attributed her death to a coronary embolism. How odd that three of his patients died of the same thing in the same year and he was in attendance at all three deaths. If anyone had taken the time to look over this pattern, alarm bells would have rang immediately. Because an embolism is a sudden attack, for a doctor to be present would actually be extremely lucky so why didn't he call an ambulance or attempt to resuscitate?

The death of Alice Gorton and the suspicious death of Jack Shelmerdine in the following year signaled another cooling off period for Shipman and he didn't kill again for almost two years after that. Because with Alice Gorton, Shipman made a terrible mistake that could have ended his career and exposed him as a murderer. He had paid a visit to Alice thinking that she would be alone, but her daughter was there with her. Shipman administered his lethal dose and coldly informed her daughter that she was dead and that there would be no need for a post-mortem. That in itself might have seemed odd, that just after death the doctor was thinking about post-mortems and telling her what to do, but then something sinister happened. The old lady groaned. Shipman had to quickly back-track

The Surgery on Market Street, Hyde, was the practice of Dr Harold Shipman, 12th October 1999.

Nicola Davies QC, the defence
in the Harold Shipman Trial,
arrives at Preston Crown Court,
12th October 1999.

Angela Woodruff, daughter of alleged victim, Kathleen Grundy, accompanied by her husband David at Preston Crown Court, 13th October 1999.

Witness Mary France at the Harold Shipman murder trial, Preston, 8th November 1999.

Witness Christine Whitworth at the Harold Shipman murder trial, Preston, 8th November 1999.

Witness Carol Chapman at the Harold Shipman murder trial, Preston, 9th November 1999. Carol was the receptionist at Dr Shipman's surgery in Hyde.

Primrose Shipman, the wife of Dr Harold Shipman arrives at Preston Crown Court to give evidence in the Shipman Inquiry, 31st January 2000.

The interior of Dr Harold Shipman's Manchester surgery, in Market Street, Hyde, 21st January 2000.

Robert Davies of the Crown Prosecution Service after Dr. Harold Shipman was found guilty, 31st January 2000.

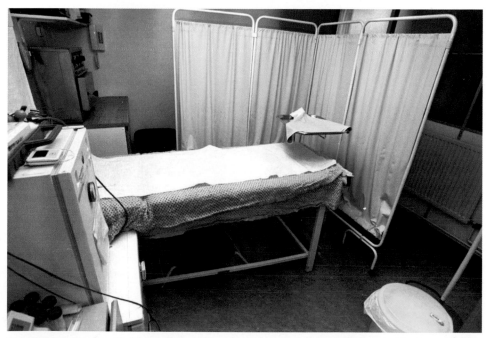

The recovery couch at Dr Harold Shipman's surgery in Hyde, Greater Manchester, 31st January 2000.

Mr Justice Forbes after the verdict in the Harold Shipman trial, 31st January 2000.

The typewriter belonging to Dr Harold Shipman which he use to forge letters and even a patient's will, 31st January 2000.

The home of Dr Harold Shipman, 1st February 2000.

The grave of Marie Quinn, one of Shipman's victims, 1st February 2000.

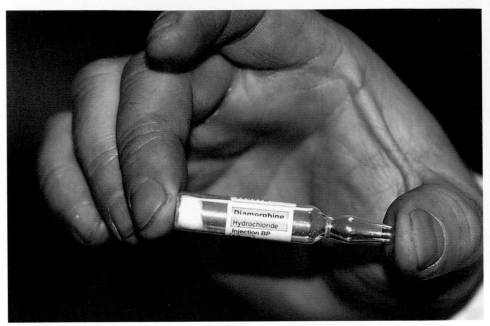

A phial of Diamorphine hydrochloride, the medical name for heroin. Dr Harold Shipman was found guilty of the murder of 15 of his patients with injections of diamorphine between March 1995 and July 1998, at Preston Crown Court.

Albert Lilly, husband of murdered Jean Lilly, sheds tears with others who lost friends and relatives to killer Harold Shipman, at a special service of prayer at St George's Church, Hyde, Greater Manchester, 1st February 2000.

on his words and pretend to fight for the poor lady's life. With the daughter present and having already witnessed him claiming she was dead when she wasn't, he could hardly raise any more suspicion. An ambulance was called and Alice Gorton slipped into a coma and died several hours later.

This incident would have shook Shipman and bruised his ego. He had got the dosage wrong and not quite killed her; what's more he had made himself look incompetent by claiming she was dead when she wasn't. Three months later, Shipman made another mistake, another lethal dose that wasn't quite enough. Jack Shelmerdine, aged seventy-seven, was visited by Shipman and, as per usual, Shipman pumped his veins with what he thought was a lethal dose of diamorphine. But Jack didn't die, he slipped into a coma and it took thirty hours for him to pass away. More worryingly for Shipman, Jack's son was irate, asking why more wasn't done to help his father. But luckily, his anger was directed towards the hospital and nobody suspected that the coma had been induced by his own GP.

These two incidents shook Shipman, and there were no more suspicious deaths recorded until April 1981. In 1981 he began to kill again and the pattern escalated: there were only two deaths the Shipman Inquiry could say were at the hands of the doctor: May Slater on 18th April and Elizabeth Ashworth on 28th November. All of his victims now followed the same MO. Elderly women (or occasionally men) living alone and suffering from some kind of condition that, whilst wasn't life threatening, could have been explained away as a possible reason for their hastened death.

The pattern of deaths continued and escalated year on year and by 1984 he was killing regularly and without the long breaks in between. Was his addiction to murder getting stronger? Just like the criminal profilers have noted – the cooling off period was getting shorter and the need to kill meant a death toll was piling up. The Shipman Inquiry looked at all of the deaths recorded by Shipman and found that, of the suspicious deaths that Shipman was most likely guilty of, the majority took place around Christmas and New Year. Could this be coincidence, or was the urge to kill stronger in the winter months? Or was it simply that older people tend to suffer from illness for in the winter due to the cold weather, slips and falls?

It wasn't until 1989 that his pattern changed and he actually killed someone in his medical practice. Eighty-one year old Mary Hamer came to visit the doctor on the 8th March. It is unknown what her complaint was, but her daughter recalls that it probably wouldn't have been that serious because she would have either called an ambulance, called her daughter, or at least told her that there was a problem. It was most likely for a routine check-up and Mrs Hamer could have been one of Shipman's 'annoying' patients that insisted on visiting the surgery regularly instead of waiting for his impromptu visits. She went into his examination room and Shipman swiftly moved her to an adjacent room where he, most likely, administered a lethal injection. While he waited for her to die, he continued to see patients, telling the receptionist that Mrs Hamer was busy undressing and it 'might take a while'.

After about thirty minutes, he went to check on Mrs Hamer and found her to be dead. He later put her cause of death as cardiac arrest; however, this was not mentioned to anyone else other than her daughter. He did not attempt to resuscitate or call an ambulance. The receptionist must have found this odd, but since this had never happened in the surgery before, and because of Shipman's superiority, no one questioned his explanation and a post-mortem was never carried out.

There was one final death that might have scared Shipman into calming his behavior, when he was nearly caught out murdering Joseph Wilcockson in 1989. A nurse discovered Wilcockson's body when it was still warm, meaning the death was extremely fresh. It is likely that she would have made a comment to Shipman, who had just visited him, asking why he had not noticed that his patient was dead, but, just like the other times before, nothing was taken any further and he got away with it.

He took nearly a year's break following this scare and it wasn't until late 1990 that two more suspicious deaths were recorded. By this time, Shipman wanted out of the Donneybrook practice. Could it have been that his colleagues were beginning to ask too many questions, beginning to wonder why he made so many house visits and why he found so many of his patients dead?

Shipman could have been responsible for more than one hundred deaths during his time at the Donnybrook practice. He worked there for a total of fourteen years and in that time there were seventy-one deaths that Shipman Inquiry concluded would have been a result of Shipman's lethal injections. On top of those deaths were another thirty suspicious deaths where there was insufficient evidence to prove whether Shipman had been involved.

By this point in his career, Shipman was a pathological serial killer. He had become so arrogant and superior that he killed as and when he liked. He had clearly developed a system of acquiring diamorphine without drawing attention to himself. Perhaps something he had learnt when he obtained huge amounts of pethidine to feed his drug habit in Todmorden.

His arrogance and egotism spread to all aspects of his life and, in 1991 he began his preparation to leave the Donneybrook practice and set up on his own. This was probably so that he could be in charge of his own patients and surgery and not have any prying eyes looking into his unusual activities.

Chapter 9

The Death Toll Rises

The Death Toll Rises

Shipman's killing pattern escalated over the years, but it wasn't until the early 1990s when he opened his own practice, that the number of the deaths rose considerably. In the three years before he was caught, Shipman killed over 100 of his own patients. What seems remarkable is that nobody seemed to notice his abnormally high mortality rate, or the fact that he was present at a huge number of deaths.

The differences between the real Shipman and his outward persona were becoming increasingly obvious, especially to his colleagues at Donneybrook Medical Centre. With his patients, he would always come across as genial and caring – making special efforts to take their calls and make house visits. However, his arrogance began to shine through when dealing with colleagues, especially those he considered beneath him. Although he did have a tendency to force through his opinion and speak questionably to support staff, he never had any real confrontations, or issues, with his fellow doctors. He chose not to mix in their social circles and rarely attended events or parties, but nobody minded; because, to everyone at the practice, Shipman came across as hard-working and conscientious, he was popular with the patients and so an asset to the surgery.

This all changed when Shipman went behind the backs of his colleagues, betraying their trust and leaving them with a huge debt of nearly £100,000 to pay. The way the surgery operated was that doctors came and went, retired or moved on and so their patient lists were left with the surgery, so that the replacement doctor could take it on. However, Shipman had other ideas. He wanted to leave Donneybrook. It could be that, as he was getting older, he was getting more set in his ways and finding it harder to act like a normal, functioning human being. His killings were getting almost out of control in terms of their frequency and obviousness. In fact, in 1990, he made two mistakes that could have drawn attention to his behaviour. He needed somewhere where he would have more freedom. Donneybrook was a large surgery with a lot of staff members; it would only take a few of them to start talking about strange things they had witnessed Shipman doing for them to start piecing together evidence.

Shipman had originally wanted to move away. This seems like a sensible move for a serial killer in a small town. The deaths were mounting and the pool of potential victims was getting smaller. He may have made vague reference to a position in Yorkshire, but nothing came of it. Perhaps it was too close to his shadowy history, or perhaps other practices where he applied had looked into his drug abuse convictions and realized that he was not supposed to be working in general practice. Whatever the reason, Shipman did not move. He chose to stay in Hyde and made the bold move of poaching thousands of patients from the Donneybrook surgery and convincing them to follow him to a new practice – one he would set up on his own.

This decision would have seemed like an immoral business move and a terrible way to treat colleagues who he had worked with for fifteen years or more; the news came as a shock to his colleagues, particular the doctors with whom he shared the financial costs of the surgery. The GPs shared the day-to-day running fees, staff wages and equipment costs. The profits of each doctor was also listed under the surgery's name, not individuals, which meant Shipman could leave with his tax-free earnings from dividends, whilst the surgery would have to pay his share of the tax bill – he had no liability. Furthermore, now Shipman was no longer a doctor at the surgery, his partners had to buy him out of his share of the building. This cost had risen with the price of inflation and, due to large sums of money needed for which the remaining doctors at Donneybrook were personally liable; they had to take out a loan to cover it. And to add insult to injury, the surgery would now be making less money because of their reduced patient list and they wouldn't be able to afford to take on anyone to replace Shipman. All in all, Shipman had abused the trust of his partners at the surgery for his own financial and personal gain. He had made enemies of his fellow doctors, yet somehow, was still popular amongst the community.

For his colleagues at Donneybrook, this was the first time they'd seen this calculating and mean side to Shipman. They may have heard rumours of how he spoke to so-called 'underlings' and sales reps, but most had enjoyed a relationship of mutual respect. The underhand way he went about leaving the surgery betrayed the image he'd built up for himself and left them all shell-shocked.

In July 1992, Shipman finally achieved what he had wanted for years – to be his own boss entirely. He set up his own surgery, imaginatively called 'The Surgery', near the centre of Hyde, close to the shops and restaurants frequented by the local community. Shipman was in an ideal situation. Unlike most serial killers who stalk their prey, or pick a particular victim, Shipman's victims came straight to him. He could easily earmark the people who he thought would slip away without question and the best thing about this selection process was that it was his job; and so he never attracted scrutiny. It wasn't long before his killing pattern emerged once again.

In 1992, the year of his surgery opening, he was careful not to attract too much attention, only killing one of his patients – Monica Sparkes, aged seventy-two. Sparkes lived in the same area of Hyde as Shipman, and it is likely that he had been monitoring Sparkes whilst easing into his transition between surgeries. Her family were aware that she was struggling with old age and cardiac problems. She had also come to the surgery a few times due to falls. Perhaps she was another of Shipman's 'problem patients' and needed eradicating. Statements from her family place Shipman in her house around three hours before her death was pronounced. He had made an unscheduled house call and whilst he was there, Mrs Sparkes' sister-in-law Phyllis Holt, called. Shipman would not let her speak to Sparkes, instead informing her that she had had a mild stroke and the ambulance was delayed. A complete lie as there was no record of Shipman calling an ambulance. It seems incredulous that her sister-in-law did not then question why Shipman left Sparkes alone, having a stroke, so that he could return to his busy surgery. When he returned that afternoon, he found her dead and called Phyllis back informing her of the death. So loved and well-respected was Shipman, that even this dubious treatment and story about the ambulance raised no suspicion and her cause of death was readily accepted.

He certainly made up for his dry spell from 1992, and in 1993, he killed at least fifteen of his patients systematically throughout the year. Like the killings in earlier years, the deaths in 1993 came in small clusters, with two in February, four between late March and April, a further four in May, two stand alone deaths over the summer and a final flourish of three in December, the final one on New Year's Eve.

By now his MO was ingrained and he rarely deviated from his pattern of visiting the victim's house armed with a lethal dose of diamorphine. He would either pronounce them dead immediately, or leave and come back later waiting to be called so he could appear the hero and feel superior in knowing A) he had caused the death and B) he was the only one with the power to pronounce it and tell others what the cause to be put on the death certificate was. He was so calculating that when investigators delved even further into the details, they noticed that in most of the cases, the central heating had been turned up very high. This meant two things: that the body would take longer to cool and that rigor mortis would set in quicker. The contraindication this created meant that it was almost impossible for the coroner to establish a time of death and so Shipman was less likely to be placed at the scene. It was certainly a sick pleasure he derived from these scenarios and with the freedom to act however he liked, he was becoming addicted.

Investigations into the Shipman murders found out just how calculating he really was. Because what Shipman didn't realise at the time, was that all of his computer entries were traceable. The forensics team in charge of sorting through all of Shipman's records found alarming anomalies. Firstly, Shipman had been devious enough to go back into patient files and alter their medical records, hinting at possible cardiac problems and even sometimes referencing a small diamorphine dose as a mild pain killer. But Shipman had been storing diamorphine. Experts tracking his movements through digital entries soon discovered that Shipman would backdate prescriptions for dead patients (usually patients he had killed) and then keep the medication for himself. Some were even collected days after the patient's death – a clear display of how far above the law he thought he was. The drug prescribed was diamorphine. They soon found a pattern of single prescriptions for 30mg ampules. Shipman would preload his syringe and then have another in stock, ready for the next victim. He had prepared in advance and was ready to kill whenever he felt like it. Acting in this way shows just how arrogant Shipman was. He was walking around every day with a blatant disregard for the same law that almost led to his downfall in Todmorden. He had been charged then for illegally possessing a controlled substance and, once again, he was walking the streets with a controlled substance. Yet nobody even questioned him; almost everyone in Hyde loved

Shipman and were desperate to get on his patient list. He had painted such an appealing picture of himself, and such a superior position within the community, that no one even considered that he might not be acting in the best interests of his patients. Nobody ever thinks that their friendly GP could be a mass murderer.

There also seems to be a clear pattern of Shipman choosing cardiac arrest or coronary embolism as a cause of death in the early 1990s. It seems logical that he would pick patients who had been suffering from heart problems, as these can be unpredictable and everyone knows how deadly a heart attack can be. Add to it that the patient supposedly suffering a heart attack was on their own, then people are less likely to question the death and why Shipman was usually the first to discover the body. Surely he was just checking on his elderly and vulnerable patient? What does seem odd is the fact that whilst he stated that many of patients died of heart problems, he also boasted around town that he was the best doctor for heart issues; he was well-known for prescribing expensive drugs to help lower cholesterol and unless people were to look into his death rates and causes, just like everything else, people accepted what he said as truth.

Shipman was flying close to the wind and his 'near misses' were increasing. First was the case of Mary Smith in August 1993, another survivor of Shipman's attacks (for now). By all accounts, Shipman was interrupted whilst administering diamorphine. Her step-daughter walked in to find Shipman calmly and closely examining Mrs Smith. But Mrs Smith was unconscious. Shipman had not said anything about giving her any drugs, so must have quickly hidden the syringe, making it look like her was tending to her. He left the house, claiming that she had passed out but would be fine and that, medically, everything was OK. He would have left not knowing whether she would live or die, depending on how she reacted to the drug. Luckily, she woke the next morning and was fine – clearly the dose was enough to send her into a deep sleep, but not enough to do any lasting damage. Shipman had evaded suspicion once again, but he was obviously shaken. As with previous situations like this, Shipman went quiet and no one died for a good few months. This pattern is reoccurring throughout Shipman's career. He was extremely good at reigning in his desire when he knew it was too dangerous to draw any more attention to himself, but how long could he keep it up?

Towards the end of November, Shipman hit the jackpot and it fuelled another killing spree. One of his patients, David Jones, was suffering from cancer and it had become terminal. Shipman actually resisted the urge to hasten his death, and instead, waited it out because there was a prize at the end. Once David had died, his excess morphine, administered by a Macmillan nurse, was left. Shipman took the responsibility of disposing of it. Once again, he was in possession of a controlled substance without the correct permissions. His authority and convincing manner meant he was able to walk away with 3,000mg of diamorphine.

Another cluster of killings followed in the December of 1993; on 16th December he killed Joseph Leigh, aged seventy-eight, on 22nd December he killed Eileen Robinson, aged fifty-four, and on the 31st of December he killed Charles Brocklehurst. Could it be that Shipman was keeping a tally, mental or otherwise of his killings. If so, he knew 1993 would be his biggest year – perhaps the murder of Charles Brocklehurst on New Year's Eve was a little nod to this 'achievement'.

For Shipman, 1993 had been a good year, his new surgery was doing well and he had a waiting list for patients. He had not only got away with at least fifteen murders in one year, he had now acquired a generous stockpile of diamorphine. He was getting a buzz from the trust and respect he had worked for in the community and all the while having ultimate control over life and death. But it wasn't long until his cockiness was getting the better of him once again. This time, it was the tragic case of Renate Overton. Despite having a large stock of diamorphine, Shipman got the dosage wrong. Shipman had initially been called to the house because Mrs Overton was struggling with a severe asthma attack. The stockpile of diamorphine must have been burning a hole in Shipman's pocket and he saw an opportunity. Shipman appeared to have calmed the attack and Mrs Overton's daughter left her alone to be checked over by Shipman. However, upon her return she discovered her mother unconscious on the kitchen floor. Shipman improvised and tried to resuscitate her – a skill he was not overly familiar with. To make it seem more convincing, he ordered the daughter to help and to also call an ambulance. Paramedics arrived on scene extremely quickly and managed to restart her heart. Unfortunately, her brain had been starved of oxygen for too long and she was left severely brain damaged, spending the rest of her short life in a permanent vegetative state. Even worse for Shipman, he had to admit to paramedics that he had given her a dose of morphine to 'ease the pain', knowing this would throw into question his competence (given the affect morphine can have on patients who suffer from breathing difficulties). It would have been clear to medical staff that her cardiac arrest would have been due to the morphine dose and some may have questioned if the attending GP had made a mistake, giving her too much. Once again, medical negligence accusations hung over Shipman. He was quick to cover his tracks; the Shipman Inquiry suggested that he would have disposed of his diamorphine stores, knowing a search would lead to another drugs conviction. As a best-case scenario he would face another drugs charge, worse still he could be struck off, or his nightmare scenario – he would be found out as a killer, rather than just a bumbling, negligent GP. Perhaps because she took fourteen months to die, staff would have been concerned with her care and any questions into Shipman's competence faded into insignificance.

He had got away with it once again, and poor Mrs Overton suffered a horrible, drawn-out death. Shortly after this incident, Shipman got rid of his visit book, which meant he no longer kept a record or when he visited patients at home – his movements could not be tracked…or so he thought.

Shipman had to go back into hiding sooner than he thought and his desire to kill would not have been satisfied. Furthermore, he had ran out of diamorphine and with the lingering death of Mrs Overton still hanging over him, he had to be careful. Shipman was a control freak and he had some unfinished business – a victim he had failed to finish off. Almost eighteen months after he'd first tried to kill Mary Smith, Shipman set his targets on her again. The need to kill must have been getting desperate; he must have known one kill would not be enough to satisfy him anymore. We can see this calculating behavior by looking back at his prescriptions. Just before returning to Mrs Smith's house (an unscheduled house call that would fail to get noted in his visit book), Shipman wrote a prescription for her for 1,000mg of diamorphine. An alarmingly high amount to hand over to a civilian; if a mistake in dosage or administering the drug were to happen, it would be enough to kill her. It would be enough to kill an elephant. Shipman took the prescription on her behalf, by now he would have had such a good relationship with the pharmacist that this raised no eyebrows. He gave Mrs Smith enough of the drug to kill her and kept the rest for himself – he had plans for the remaining supply. He killed throughout the summer of 1994; the only confirmed deaths by the Shipman Inquiry are: Ronnie Davenport, aged fifty-seven; Cicely Sharples, aged eighty-seven; Alice Kitchen, aged seventy and Maria Thornton, aged seventy-eight. However, it is likely that Shipman killed far more than that because he had to replenish his diamorphine stocks twice – once with 500mg and again with 1,000mg. He would have only needed a fraction of that to kill four more people after Mary Smith. At a push he might only use

100mg for each person. So where did the other 2,000mg go? In the arms of unknown victims, victims he did a better job of covering up on?

Unbelievably, Shipman was just warming up. He had a new, foolproof way of obtaining diamorphine and an addiction to killing off his patients that was getting out of hand. How long would it be until someone noticed his shockingly high mortality rates?

In 1995, Shipman committed mass murder on a tremendous scale. There were twenty-eight deaths that the Shipman Inquiry found to be the result of a lethal overdose. The pattern continued, with patients falling every other week. Murdering patients was now part of Shipman's routine. He'd become so entrenched in his own pathology that it would have been almost impossible for him to stop. It had become a psychological problem and something he was no longer in control of. His obsessive nature forced him to act out the ritual again and again; he was convincing himself he was in control of feeding his desire, but by now he was a loose cannon.

1996 saw the deaths of thirty more victims; these being the ones that the Shipman Inquiry could definitely say were the work of Shipman. But how many more might have slipped through the net? By 1997, the killings were increasing with almost one a week and 1998 saw a new flurry of deaths, starting in mid January. They continued until Shipman's last victim, Kathleen Grundy, was killed 24th June 1998. By this point, Shipman had killed eighteen people that year already and around 250 people in total. During the last three years of Shipman's reign, his MO changed slightly. By now he had killed over 140 people. Perhaps, initially, he had got a kick out of watching people die, but this was probably getting boring, perhaps he was so blasé he couldn't be bothered to wait, or perhaps his presence at so many deaths was becoming suspicious. So, instead of administering an injection that caused immediate death, Shipman changed his tack – he started to inject his victims slower, meaning that where deaths used to take a couple of minutes, they now took a couple of hours. This gave him time to flee the scene and either have no connection to the death whatsoever, or be called in as the hero doctor by grieving relatives.

How do we know this? There is one key witness that can give us an insight into the doctor's killing routine. Ann Smith spoke to her dying aunt on the phone and confirmed this theory. Shipman had visited seventy-year-old Lucy Virgin on 1st March 1995, which would have been just at the beginning of this new, absence-style MO. Lucy had visited the surgery with a minor complaint only a few weeks prior to her attack. Shipman then made an unscheduled visit 'just to check up', giving her a slower injection of morphine than was usual for his victims – he also gave her a packet of antibiotics, an alibi for his presence there, and may have told her that the injection was related to this. He left her in her home whilst she was still conscious. This was a dangerous move and one that backfired. Lucy was still awake enough to get up and call her niece, and what she told her gives us a unique insight into the actions of Shipman. She told her niece that the doctor had called to check up on her and that he had given her an injection. She also said that the doctor had instructed her not to go anywhere. Little did she know that it was because he had left her to die, alone and oblivious to her fate. Ann Smith played a bigger part in her aunt's death than she realized, because Shipman had actually preplanned her death with one of Ann's regular visits to the surgery. He had realized that discovering so many bodies himself would start to look weird. He planted the tiniest of seeds, simply asking if she'd seen her aunt, perhaps implying that she was not well. This was enough to prompt Ann to call Lucy. After no response, she went to the house and found her dead body.

Ann called Dr Shipman and then an ambulance. Shipman arrived first. He was quick to bamboozle Ann with her aunt's death, insinuating that she needed to make decisions immediately about cremation and a post-mortem. He was also swift to announce the cause of death, having barely examined her. Ann, the niece, was prepped ready for the arrival of the paramedics. She remembers Shipman being cold and indifferent to death and assumed that he was unaffected by it because he was a doctor, not a psychopath.

For Shipman, Lucy's case was a learning experience in dosage, just like the early experiments with pethidine it is thought he carried out on his patients in Pontefract. He now knew he needed to administer enough to incapacitate the victim, but not too much that they died in his presence. A fine balance and one he perfected.

By now, Shipman had killed a lot of people and like all addicts, he was not getting the same buzz from just one kill. His escalation pattern follows that of any serial killer, just on a much larger scale. More than likely this was down to the ease in which he could find and then murder his victims. Whilst he is famous as a 'granny killer', it seems Shipman's choice of victim was indiscriminate and he would kill to suit his own needs. Most would have been opportunistic. By the mid to late 1990s, Shipman was probably killing around once a week, or once every other week. He would no doubt select his victims from people who had recently visited him, ear-marking them for extinction should they show a sign of weakness that could easily explain away their death. However, the case of Arthur Stopford is an interesting one. Looking back at faked medical records, we can see that Shipman was now having to invent fake illnesses for his patients so that he could get extra diamorphine. In Arthur's case, he had queried a cancer diagnosis and prescribed diamorphine. However, his family became suspicious when Arthur had not been referred for biopsy and there was no treatment plan in place. The family were an obstruction Shipman didn't need and Arthur died soon after.

He also varied his method, occasionally taking the opportunity to kill patients in his own surgery. He had only done this once at Donneybrook, but now there were no prying eyes and no rubber-necking receptionists to worry about. The first to go was Joan Harding. Her death must have seemed suspicious to friends, as she went in fit and healthy and came out in a body bag. Shipman, as usual, put it down to a massive heart attack, "It could have happened at any time," he said.

The next victim came eighteen months later – the time gap shows Shipman was being careful. Betty (Bertha) Moss was another seemingly healthy lady, she had an existing heart problem but was well enough to walk to the shops and socialize with friends. She combined her visit to the surgery with a trip to the market, a shopping trip she never got to finish. Shipman was escalating, feeding off this new buzz and it wasn't long before he killed again. This time it was Dora Ashton, who was well enough to walk to the surgery for a routine check. Shipman's next surgery kill fits with the theory that he bumped off patients he considered to be a nuisance – he disliked frequent visits and would prefer to make house calls; a power trip, or a deadly intention? Edith Brady was a regular to the surgery, so much so her family joked about the frequency of her visits. Shipman soon put an end to her enthusiasm for the doctor's waiting room and she left in a body bag.

Shipman's surgery killings were to come to an abrupt end when, once again, he nearly attracted the wrong kind of attention. Ivy Lomas, Shipman's final surgery victim has many similarities with the one person he killed in his time at Donneybrook. She was a frequent visitor and he would often make snide comments about her being a permanent fixture in his waiting room. The other similarity is that he killed her with a lethal injection, leaving her to die in a separate room whilst he saw three other patients, exactly the same thing he had done before. Had he timed it? Shipman was caught out with Lomas, because unbeknownst to him, none of her family were able to be tracked down. He was busy seeing patients so his receptionist took matters into her own hands and called the police. The police were shocked that he had not attempted to resuscitate her, but Shipman managed to talk his way around it using his medical knowledge and academic superiority as a shield. Although he got away with this murder, he probably knew that it had been a close call, especially if the police officers had decided to treat it as a suspicious death. Just over a year after her death, Shipman had been caught and, because her family had opted for a burial, this meant that her body could be exhumed and examined. Shipman was later convicted of her murder in 2000.

Shipman was perfecting his kills with every fresh victim. He was getting adept at cremation forms and implying others were present at the death, or that people had seen the victims alive following his visits. He was still well-respected and loved within the community. He was in the perfect position; as their doctor nobody would suspect that he wanted to kill them and he was usually the first contact when people found a body. He was a person to turn to and the vulnerable and grieving relatives would believe his every word. He'd use their most vulnerable moments to force through cremation papers, avoiding the risk of a post-mortem later on and, because he was familiar with their medical records, he was able to pronounce a cause of death that people were unlikely to question. Who knew better the reason for the victim's death than their own doctor?

In the summer of 1996, Shipman faked a prescription for 12,000mg of diamorphine. A tremendous amount of opiates that bizarrely went unnoticed. He embarked on a killing spree that summer, taking the lives of five people in July and it seems that the only reason the killing stopped is because Shipman took a holiday. Was murder becoming his full time job? He was so popular in the town that he had a waiting list for patients. Perhaps flicking the elderly from the top was just an elaborate way of house-keeping, of making way for less troublesome, younger people.

But Shipman's world was getting smaller, he was operating in a small town and he'd killed off so many people that the remaining victims all knew someone who had died in a similar way to their recently deceased relative. Shipman was spinning a tangled web, telling lies and half-truths that, should people talk, might reveal his true nature. He even made a slip up with the undertakers: pre-empting people he would need to eradicate over Christmas, he asked for cremation forms for patients he thought might die over the festive season. This must have seemed very odd and even more so, when the undertakers received a call informing them of the deaths – how could Shipman have predicted their deaths so accurately?

Could it have been the case that Shipman was spiraling out of control? His lies were beginning to catch up with him and his victim pool was starting to look murky. He would have to watch his step and think ahead. He had an insatiable desire to kill and his murders were becoming more and more suspicious and conspicuous. What were his choices? Perhaps, by now, he was being controlled by his urges and had finally reached the acceptance stage. It was time to regain control.

The Death Toll Rises

Chapter 10

Found Out

Found Out

Angela Woodruff, the daughter of Shipman's final victim, Kathleen Grundy, brought Shipman's reign of terror to an end. Angela's investigations and persistence put Shipman and his numerous deaths in the spotlight. He had forged Grundy's will, which was a deviation from his modus operandi and eventually led to his arrest. What we'll never know is – did he want to get caught?

Criminologists who have studied serial killers believe that the typical serial killer, if not caught, will continue murdering for around thirty years. Some simply retire and are never caught, whilst others choose to go out in a blaze of glory. Shipman had been killing for over thirty years, but it had only significantly escalated from the mid-eighties, with an unprecedented numbers of deaths piling up once he opened his own practice. Were the huge numbers of deaths signalling a final flourish, or pointing towards a deranged psychopath spiralling out of control? It is unlikely Shipman would have had enough self-awareness to recognize the gravity of what he was doing. Just like a compulsive liar believes their own lies, Shipman had probably convinced himself that this was just the way he did his job. He had such a high opinion of himself that he may have felt justified in taking people's lives.

Working as the sole practitioner, in a small town with adoring patients, it is easy for an ego to inflate out of all proportion. With no colleagues to ground him and an ever-increasing sense of superiority, Shipman must have felt like he was beyond reproach. His fellow doctors in the area found his arrogance irritating to the point of being embarrassing.

Shipman's patients, however, formed a different opinion to his peers. To them, he was helpful and caring and an extremely good GP. He would always fight for the best treatment for his patients; he would listen to their problems and didn't seem to judge them. In fact, when he first set up his practice, a loyal patient, Len Fallows offered to help out. Together, Fallows and Shipman set up a 'Patient Fund'. It was like a co-operative fundraising scheme, whereby patients could help other patients. Donations to the fund would go back into the surgery and be used to buy much needed equipment, such as testing kits, ECG monitors, even a foetal heart detector. The cynical critics may suggest that Shipman was hiding behind the guise of charity in order to kit out his own surgery with top-of-the-range equipment – because having better facilities meant more patients. And a constant waiting list fed Shipman's ego. There is no evidence to suggest that any of these funds were diverted away from the intended purpose. Perhaps Shipman had some kind of moral code he adhered to? Or perhaps staying above board on this helped maintain the persona he had built up for himself. It was just another way to divert attention away from his criminal activities.

He certainly wasn't above taking from his patients; Shipman soon discovered an added bonus to killing people who trusted and respected him – they left him money in their wills. Shipman may have talked to them, convinced them to sign over some money to him, so that it could be invested into the 'Patient Fund' – like a way of preserving a legacy after death by helping your community with extra health care. Or perhaps they had chosen to bequeath him money of their own accord, just because they appreciated his help. Either way, Shipman started to inherit small sums of money from his victims. But he went further, stealing from their houses. When police raided his house following his arrest, they found lots of small items of jewellery, pieces that would be too small for Primrose (because Primrose, by this stage in life, had ballooned in size). Some families also reported missing cash from the houses. Clearly, Shipman had no morals with regard to stealing from his dead patients and so it seems more likely that the reason he didn't embezzle funds from his own charity was so as not to attract suspicion to any of his activities. It seems strange that a GP, working as a sole practitioner, would need to steal jewellery and petty cash. He earned a massive salary and was living in the modest house he had bought when he first moved to Hyde in the 1970s. Whilst some believe he sold the jewellery to pawn brokers, it is more likely that these steals were trophies; so that when his buzz was waning, he could look at his stash of stolen costume jewellery, or feel smug buying a coffee with his murder victim's spare change.

The occasional patient leaving him money in their will set cogs turning inside Shipman's brain. Whether he had grown tired of the constant killing and was genuinely looking for a way to retire and disappear, or whether he wanted to get caught – getting a big pay out from a will was Shipman's next challenge. Was it a new way to get a buzz, a new pattern of escalation? Whatever it was, it was one final step too far.

Kathleen Grundy's will was Shipman's undoing, but he had actually tried it previously. His first target was Bianka Pomfret, aged forty-nine. Pomfret was originally from Germany, but had moved to the UK in the 1970s after meeting and marrying a British soldier. Despite her young age, Pomfret was deeply unwell. She suffered from mental health problems and visited Shipman regularly, some say almost every week. She had come to think of Shipman as her saviour; he showed her kindness and patience and never judged her. For Shipman, she was the ideal person to manipulate, a vulnerable lady whose mental health issues he knew well and knew how to handle to his advantage.

She had now divorced the soldier, Adrian, and her son had married and was getting on with his own life. She was alone, or so Shipman thought, and he was the strongest influence over her fragile mind.

Pomfret was so enamoured with Shipman that she had left him almost everything she owned, an estate that amounted to around £60,000. But Shipman had not counted on Adrian, her ex-husband, still being in the picture. Adrian still cared for Pomfret and they had remained friends following their divorce. She had told him of her plans and, luckily, Adrian had managed to talk some sense into her. He convinced her that her son and grandchildren would be far better beneficiaries. Pomfret changed her will again in November 1997 leaving her estate to her son.

On 10th December 1997, Shipman visited Pomfret at her house. That day she had already called the surgery twice, although no one can be sure what the nature of the calls were. Because Pomfret was suffering from mental health problems, she had other visitors besides Shipman. This is not something he would have necessarily known about, but if he did, he certainly didn't care. Support workers and a psychiatrist had visited Pomfret on the days leading up to her death. When questioned later, they remember her being in good health and managing her illness well. But Shipman believed he was above it all and visited her in the afternoon, ready to force through his inheritance. He injected her with a lethal dose of diamorphine and left her on her sofa. He may have even offered to make her a drink, as witnesses at the ensuing scene of her death report seeing a half-empty mug of coffee. Later that afternoon, another of Pomfret's support workers called by; there was no response at the door, but she could see through the window that Pomfret was in and started to worry. The support worker called her son (most-likely listed as her next of kin) and he came to the house with spare keys. They let themselves in and found her dead body. An ambulance crew was called and then, Shipman. Bold as brass, Shipman strode in and proceeded to announce her cause of death – coronary thrombosis and heart disease. This was shocking news to the family and the first they had heard of any heart problems. Shipman assured them that he knew her medical history better than they did and that she did, indeed, suffer from angina. Little did they know that Shipman had made this up completely. After confirming her death, he returned to his surgery and inputted ten months' worth of false medical records. Shipman was unaware that his computer system ran a tracking program in the background of its operating system. Detectives would later analyse the entries to prove that he had falsified hundreds of medical records. Pomfret's family was deeply shocked by her sudden death. Forty-nine was very young to die of a heart condition, especially one that had showed no previous warning signs. Her son took this up with Shipman. But Shipman was prepared and full of righteous indignation. He had already told them once that there was no need for a post-mortem, he had visited the patient hours before her death, he knew of her medical history and he was qualified to confirm a cause of death.

Shipman would have been sorely disappointed to discover that Pomfret had changed her will again, removing him from it. He had failed. If this was a new part of his sick game, he had got off to a bad start. But just like the early experiments with pethidine, and the teething problems he faced when changing his MO, perhaps this was just another learning experience for Shipman. Six months later, he had succeeded, or so he thought, in inheriting a large sum of money – the benefactor was his final victim, Kathleen Grundy, who was eighty-one.

Shipman changed approach, going one step further this time; he took it upon himself to forge Kathleen's will without her knowledge. However, unaware of the legal procedure surrounding a will, he did not do a very good job of it. Shipman had a typewriter and, in the weeks before he killed Kathleen Grundy, he set about forging her will. First he needed her compliance so that he could obtain her signature. From information given to police by friends and relatives, it seems Shipman obtained her signature by feeding her lies. He told her that he'd like to enter her into a study at Manchester University, flattering her by saying it was about aging and she would be perfect because she was so fit and healthy for her age. He produced bogus forms for her to sign; little did she know she was signing a request to amend her own will.

Next, he needed signatures of witnesses, and this is where his boldness and convincing manner goes beyond belief. Shipman had either orchestrated that two ideal witnesses be in his waiting room at the same time, or he had such self-belief that he popped his head round the corner to see who he could use. Shipman called upon Paul Spencer and Claire Hutchinson. Paul remembered how he had been sat in the GP's waiting room, waiting to see the doctor for a repeat prescription of antibiotics. He recalled details about Shipman's character, how he was genial and always made an effort to remember little details about each patient, so as to make them feel cared for. Whilst he was waiting, Claire Hutchinson was also sat in the doctor's waiting room.

Shipman now had the change of will prepared, but he wouldn't be able to send it until after Grundy had died, because otherwise the solicitors might want to check with her and she would deny the change. Now all Shipman needed to do was kill her. He visited her house on 24th June 1998 and, as with all his other victims, administered a lethal dose of diamorphine. True to his new MO, he then stayed away and waited for the call. It wasn't long before two friends discovered the body and Shipman was called to the scene. He quickly examined Grundy, more than likely a show for the friends, and then pronounced her death, stating she had died of a cardiac arrest. Not used to dealing with death, the two friends were unsure of what to do next and so consulted Dr Shipman, asking his advice on how best to proceed. Shipman said that they should contact her solicitors at a law firm in Hyde, Hamilton Ward; it may have seemed strange at the time that Shipman knew who her solicitors were, but the men trusted their local doctor and followed his instructions.

The friends were unable to contact her daughter and so the police were called. Shipman remained calm and explained away Grundy's death without raising any initial suspicion. Shipman left Grundy's house, thinking that he was in control of the situation. He then back-dated and posted Grundy's change of will to the solicitors in Hyde.

The police were able to track down Kathleen Grundy's daughter, Angela, and broke the news of her mother's death. A devastated Angela and her husband, David Woodruff, set off for Hyde first thing the following morning. After arriving in Hyde, Angela met with Dr Shipman to discuss the circumstances of her mother's death. Angela recalls Shipman's persona being somewhat cold and unsympathetic, completely unlike the character he had been described as by Kathleen and other members of the Hyde community.

In the typewritten change of will, forged by Shipman, Grundy had requested to be cremated. However, the solicitors did not look into the will until after the funeral. Angela knew that her mother had wanted to be buried and, much to Shipman's dismay, Grundy's body was buried and not cremated.

When the solicitors informed Angela of her mother's change of will, they were all just as shocked. Shipman had not counted on the fact the Angela was a solicitor herself and was well aware of what her mother's actual will should have looked like, because she helped her to write it. By this point, Shipman must have been panicking a little. So, as to make her request seem more convincing, he dug himself an even bigger hole – he forged a second letter (also typewritten) by someone claiming to be a friend of Kathleen Grundy's. The letter was from a made-up person by the name of Joel Smith. It explained that he had helped Grundy to type out her amended will and it also informed the solicitors of Grundy's death. Was Shipman really that arrogant to think that the solicitors would take the word of two typewritten letters, one from a person who could not be traced? Shipman had even used the name Joel, the street name where Grundy lived. Perhaps he was tired and unimaginative – this fits his laziness in pronouncing causes of death and blasé attitude to acquiring drugs; or could it be he was continually pushing the envelope, seeing how obvious he could be until somebody took notice. Was he playing with the authorities? Goading them into noticing him?

Angela certainly noticed and she could not accept a will that now left the entirety of her mother's estate (which totaled around £400,000) to her GP. The solicitors were also dubious and put a freeze on the funds, pending further investigation. At this point, it was still a civil matter and the worst crime that Shipman was remotely suspected of was forging Grundy's will, and even that was a bold accusation to make. Angela needed proof.

Angela embarked upon her own investigation, first finding the co-signers of her mothers altered will. It wasn't hard to connect the two witnesses to Shipman, since they both remembered signing the document (even if they didn't know what they were signing) in his office. She may have even been suspicious about her mother's death; now she was convinced that Shipman had forged her mother's will in order to steal her inheritance, she now began to wonder – had he ended her life to achieve this?

She passed her concerns onto the police, initially asking for them to investigate it as a case of fraud. Had one particular detective not been working this case, Shipman may well have got away with Grundy's murder, and would have only been charged with fraud. Luckily, Detective Inspector Egerton remembered the name Shipman. A few years ago, a local GP had raised concerns about Shipman's abnormally high mortality rate. This had been dismissed as a one-off comment, but now it had made Egerton think. Could Shipman have killed Kathleen Grundy?

Egerton sought advice from his superior, Detective Chief Superintendent Bernard Postles. Postles authorized Egerton's request to have Kathleen Grundy's body exhumed. But that was not all; the Greater Manchester Police were about to launch a full-scale investigation into all of the deaths recorded by Shipman in the past year. This would turn out to be one of the biggest investigations in British history, involving forensics teams, computer experts, as well as combined resources from fraud, homicide and drugs divisions. They soon realized that if their worst fears were confirmed, they would need victim support coordinators and bereavement teams on hand for the relatives.

Kathleen Grundy's body was exhumed on 1st August 1998. After her body was raised from the ground, it was sent to forensic pathologist, John Rutherford. The police knew the results would take a long time and they needed to act fast. They obtained search warrants for both Shipman's surgery and home. Two search teams arrived simultaneously, as part of a plan to prevent Shipman hiding or destroying any evidence. At this point, Shipman still thought that he had covered his tracks so he was happy to let the police search his home and office – he even handed over the typewriter, admitting to helping Grundy with her will. Later SOCOs would match Shipman's fingerprints to the typewriter and to the supposed will of Kathleen Grundy, however, none of Grundy's fingerprints were ever found on either the typewriter or the will.

Shipman probably thought that the police wouldn't be able to prove anything and he had made sure of this by altering Grundy's medical records, insinuating she had a drug abuse problem – a lie he hoped would explain the diamorphine that the forensic pathologist was sure to discover. But Shipman still had not realized that his entries into the computer system could be tracked and date-stamped – something that would later be proof of his calculating behavior.

Meanwhile, detectives had seized a year's worth of death certificates and were beginning to trawl through the paperwork. They highlighted any suspicious deaths by certain criteria. The process was long and laborious and involved speaking to relatives just coming to terms with the death of a loved one. But they needed information. They flagged any deaths where the family said that it had come as a shock; they then cross-referred the causes of death against the medical records, looking for inconsistencies; they also used top computer analysts, as well as hand-writing analysts to determine whether a patient's medical records had been altered after the initial entry. If the body had been buried rather than cremated, and fitted the criteria above, it became a top priority.

The police flagged a great many of deaths as 'suspicious', but they ran into problems. In a lot of cases the families were not interested – for them the grief was too raw and they simply wanted to move on. Others would have heard what was going on and still placed their trust in Shipman, not wanting to believe that he could have killed their relative. In the end, they narrowed it down to fourteen cases that they needed to investigate further.

At first, Shipman was polite and compliant. As the investigations continued, the local community began to realize the severity of the situation. However, most people still would not believe that Shipman was capable of murder, or even fraud for that matter. There was a great deal of sympathy amongst the townsfolk. Shipman was proactive, even holding his own press conference to deflect negative attention and suspicions. The community rallied around Shipman, refusing to believe he could possibly have murdered his own patient and forged her will to disinherit her own family for his own financial gain. Shipman may have been aware that he had at least a little bit of breathing room as toxicology reports take time and a definitive cause of death could take up to a month to come through. Shipman barely bothered to protest his innocence and rather chose to shrug off the matter implying to friends and colleagues that they would find 'not so much as aspirin'. His supporters never faltered, trusting their local GP so much that they did not even entertain the idea that he might be responsible for the death of an innocent old lady. The local community resented the large police presence in their town, claiming that Shipman was being unfairly targeted and victimized. Whilst some could not even accept that he had played any part in the deaths, others believed that if it were the case, he was only doing it out of mercy – to help those suffering from terminal illness. No doubt, excuses Shipman had already suggested to the occasional sympathetic ear, knowing news of his plight and unfair treatment would spread throughout the town. But even the support of an entire community could not protect Shipman.

The press showed little to no interest to begin with – only the Manchester Evening News ran a small story on the unusual events following the death of an old lady. However, news of the investigation spread and soon newspapers all over the world wanted to know what was going on. This posed a massive problem for the police. If any witness spoke to the press, they could be discredited in court and it could bring down their entire case. They didn't have to fend off the media for too much longer; on 2nd September, the toxicology report came back from Grundy's body. The forensics team could now confirm that Grundy's real cause of death was a lethal overdose of morphine. The police finally had enough evidence to arrest Shipman, and on 7th September, he was arrested after voluntarily agreeing to come to Ashton-under-Lyne police station. He arrived with his solicitor, Ann Ball, who was probably unaware of the extent to which Shipman's crimes stretched. He was charged with murder, theft and forgery and was remanded in custody overnight.

But the ordeal was far from over, for both Shipman and the police. Now, fourteen more bodies needed to be exhumed.

Chapter 11

Exhumations

Exhumations

Twelve exhumations were carried out in total, revealing the gruesome truth about Shipman's activities. Lethal quantities of morphine were found in the tissue of each victim's body. Despite the public interest and worldwide news coverage by this point, the media were unable to get footage of the late night grave digging, as every time a body was lifted from the ground – police shone floodlights towards the cameras, giving the dead and their grieving families a small amount of privacy.

There were twelve exhumations that were authorised by the Shipman investigation. Following the initial exhumation of Kathleen Grundy, the forensic reports, plus the preliminary investigations into Shipman's dead patients, gave the police enough evidence to suspect Shipman had killed more than just one of his patients.

The second exhumation took place two weeks after the exhumation of Kathleen Grundy's body. On 21st September 1998, the body of Joan Melia was pulled from the ground. She was of particular interest to the police, because she ticked all the boxes in terms of suspicion surrounding her death: her death had come out of the blue to family and friends, she had been fit and active before she died, her medical records were inconsistent with her cause of death and appeared inconsistent according to analysts. Joan was described by friends and family as fit and healthy and did not look her age (73). A key witness in Joan's case was her partner, Derek Steele, whom Shipman may not have known existed. She visited the surgery on the day of her death, 12th June 1998, with a minor complaint and a tickly cough. So when she came out with a diagnosis of pneumonia, Derek was shocked.

He later spoke to police about his concerns that day – if she was so ill, why hadn't she been sent to hospital, and why had she only been given antibiotics? It was these inconsistencies that helped police realize Shipman was lying and that her death was unlikely to have been natural. Joan seemed fine to Derek, so he returned her home, where she still lived alone. We now know that Shipman called round to Joan's house a few hours later and administered a lethal injection, placing her in an armchair to be found later. But he picked the wrong chair; when Derek called round at 5pm, he found Joan dead – but what surprised him was that she was sat in the armchair. He told police that she never sat in the armchair because it was reserved for guests – she preferred the sofa. The inconsistencies were adding up. Just like other trusting members of the community, Derek called Dr Shipman; Shipman didn't even bother to examine Joan Melia, instead he simply announced that she was now dead.

The discovery of morphine in Melia's body tissue was the smoking gun detectives needed and it hinted towards a pattern of killing. This finding meant they had evidence to back up a request to unearth more bodies – bodies they suspected of being Shipman's murder victims. The third exhumation was that of Winifred Mellor, as with the previous two victims, high levels of morphine were found in her tissue, inconsistent with her medical records and her supposed cause of death. Winifred Mellor was also seventy-three, she was a widow, Shipman's ideal candidate, but she still led a busy life and spoke regularly to each of her five children. Friends remember her being in good health that day and she had taken a trip into town to shop around the market. Mellor's next-door neighbour became another crucial witness for the police. She remembers Shipman arriving at her house around 3pm and then again at 6.30pm. Shipman may or may not have known that his first visit had been noticed, but it is likely that he did not care – he was above question. On his second visit, Shipman went to the neighbour's house and asked for a key, because he could not get an answer. Blinded by concern, she unquestioningly led Shipman into Mellor's house where they found Winifred's dead body. The neighbour remembers Shipman performing a quick and heartless examination of Mellor, showing no signs of compassion. Prompted by the neighbour, Shipman called Mellor's daughter, Kathleen, to break the news. He also added an extra lie – that she had called him and asked him to come back because she was feeling unwell. When police looked into this, there was no record of such a call. Shipman left and returned later that evening when Kathleen was there; he had just left the body in the chair. Mellor's priest was also there and remembers Shipman's unprofessional and harsh approach. He tried to force through his recommendations for undertakers and cremation. He had given the cause of death as a cardiac arrest, backing it up with the claim that she was suffering from angina and refusing treatment. He insinuated that Mellor had brought the death on herself and seemed annoyed at this. Police would later discover that Shipman had gone back into Mellor's medical files and constructed a false history of heart disease. He later denied visiting earlier that day, despite eyewitness accounts from the neighbours.

Shipman would not have been aware at the time, but by now the evidence was becoming damning. Next came the exhumation of Bianka Pomfret, whose family Shipman had tried to defraud out of their inheritance. At the last minute Pomfret had changed her mind and, instead of bequeathing her estate to Shipman, she saw sense and left it to her family. Shipman had manipulated Pomfret, who suffered from mental illness into almost willingly handing over her estate to her doctor rather than her family. Like Winifred Mellor, Shipman had created a fake history of angina to back up claims he would later make on the death certificate, and to her family, that she had died of a heart attack. Shipman had abused the power he had in denoting a cause of death and advising on post-mortems. He was in the ideal position to cover his own tracks. Even when the family questioned her history of heart problems, and why she hadn't been treated in hospital (especially as she spent a lot of time in hospitals anyway), Shipman used his position as a doctor to force through his opinion: because he knew best and he knew more about her medical history than they did. When police heard from Pomfret's ex-husband about the debacle with her will, combined with stories from other families of missing money and jewellery, they were starting to see a bigger picture emerge.

Soon the exhumation of buried bodies became a common occurrence in Hyde. Marie Quinn and Ivy Lomas followed shortly after Pomfret. Marie Quinn was another active old lady, and a member of the same church as Bianka Pomfret. The case of Marie Quinn's death gave police an even better insight into Shipman's MO. Shipman arrived at her house and, on this occasion, he killed her immediately – perhaps he couldn't be bothered to return in the unpleasant weather. But unfortunately, it wasn't as clean cut as he had hoped – the undertakers were busy and he had to come back later that evening to sort out the body. Shipman recounted a story that, no doubt, he had told several times already – of an old woman calling him for help and when he arrived she was dead or dying. But the undertaker, Debbie Massey, remembers one strange coincidence from another story he had told her. In both stories, Shipman had told the victim to leave the door unlocked, so he could let himself him. He would also do this when leaving a body for the undertakers, so he did not have to bother coming back to answer questions about the death. Massey found it strange that Shipman had called them more than once to a scene like this, something no other doctor had done.

Ivy Lomas was different from Shipman's usual MO, he killed her in his surgery. She was a typical 'problem patient' in Shipman's eyes and would always be at the surgery with some minor complaint. She sat patiently in the waiting room, displaying no signs of discomfort. Shipman led her through to a consulting room and killed her. Her left her alone for around thirty minutes whilst he saw other patients; he then came back out and announced, to the receptionist, that she had died, making up some deflecting story about an ECG machine at the same time. Medical professionals who have looked back on the five deaths that occurred in Shipman's practice have noted that this is very odd indeed. It is very uncommon for someone to die in a doctor's surgery. Shipman had put down Lomas' cause of death as cardiac arrest, but if a patient had come to the GP surgery experiencing chest pains, then an ambulance would have been called immediately. There was no record of Shipman calling for an ambulance, negligence he could not explain away later when questioned by police.

On the 10th, 11th and 12th of November, Irene Turner, Alice Kitchen and Jean Lilley were pulled from their graves respectively. Irene Turner had just returned from a holiday in Devon when Shipman visited her home. She was later found laid out on her bed, but not how you would expect someone to be if they were sleeping or had just suffered a heart attack. The abnormally high levels of morphine in Turner's body shocked toxicologists; Shipman must have injected her with so much diamorphine that she died within minutes. This would have given him time to lay out her body and roam around her house looking for trophies of his kill. Later, when friends and relatives spoke to the police, they found inconsistencies in Shipman's story. To a neighbour he had said that Mrs Turner needed to go to hospital, that a bed was ready for her and that she might need help packing some things. This was clearly a rouse, just so that the neighbour would discover the body. But Shipman changed his story with Turner's son-in-law, saying that she had refused to go to hospital. Unfortunately, these inconsistencies were not discovered until the police investigated over two years later.

Alice Kitchen was killed on 17th June 1994. Just like all of his other victims, she had seemed fine earlier in the day. Her son, Mick, was a taxi driver and had left her at home around lunchtime. He returned later that afternoon to find her dead, slumped over on the sofa (a neighbour later told police that she never sat there, always preferring the chair, so she could look out of the window). Mick was shocked by the discovery, but it wasn't all he discovered: he also found a note left by Shipman. The note was written at 4pm, or so Shipman claimed, and said that Alice had suffered a mild stroke, but had refused to go to hospital because she knew Mick would be returning soon. This seemed very lazy on Shipman's part and Alice's neighbour was quite upset when she learned of this – if she had known, she would have gone round to look after Alice until Mick arrived. This seemed like a rather uncaring act and the family even considered taking action against Shipman for neglect. Mick called Shipman back around to the house to confirm the death. He was obviously unhappy with the care she had received, but Shipman managed to talk his way around it, blaming it on Alice for being belligerent and negating the issue by saying that had she have gone to hospital, she would have died from the 'second stroke' anyway.

Jean Lilley was the perfect potential victim and Shipman would have been alerted to this fact during her routine visits to the surgery. She suffered from heart disease as well as breathing problems, so she would fit neatly into a open and shut case of cardiac arrest, even despite her pre-geriatric age of fifty-eight. Shipman visited her on 25th April 1997 with a lethal dose of diamorphine. Her sudden death, whilst tragic, did not come as a complete shock to her family. They readily accepted Shipman's given cause of death and it was only when the toxicology reports came back that they started to suspect him of foul play.

By now the police had enough evidence and witness statements to establish a clear MO, but now they wanted to find out just how far back they could go and still find physical evidence of Shipman's crimes – the research certainly suggested that he had been doing this for years. The final three exhumations took place in December 1998. Sarah Ashworth came out first, and was the oldest of Shipman's victims to be exhumed; she had died in 1993 and the coffin and corpse were in a severe state of decay. Ashworth was a widow and a potential early cash cow for Shipman. She had assets worth over £1 million and the power of killing of rich, old ladies may have set cogs turning in his twisted mind. Ashworth kept to herself and was a heavy smoker, so her death did not come as a great surprise. Due to the severe decay in Ashworth's tissue, it was impossible for the toxicologists to find a definitive cause of death. However, even the slightest presence of morphine almost six years after death, would have been enough in the mind of some. This exhumation meant that there was a limit to how far back the police could go. They realized that there was no point in looking back any further and should concentrate on more recent deaths.

The last two bodies to be pulled out were Muriel Grimshaw, on the 8th of December, and Elizabeth Mellor on the 9th. Grimshaw was an active seventy-six-year old, who socialized with friends and family quite regularly. She had attended church the day before she died and had seemed in good health to everyone she met. In Muriel Grimshaw's case, it seems Shipman kept his deadly visit to her a secret, unlike most cases where he openly admitted visiting a patient in the hours prior to their death. Perhaps he thought a pattern would emerge and that he was becoming too obvious. If no one had seen him, then no one needed to know he was ever there. Grimshaw's daughter discovered her mother's body the day after she had died, after making several phone calls and getting no response. After discovering the body, her daughter called their trusted GP, Dr Shipman. Shipman arrived, in another change to his MO, with a trainee nurse. He informed the daughter that Muriel Grimshaw had suffered a stroke and died. He had even staged the room so that the TV was on, the curtains were left open and she was fully clothed, but on the bed. Shipman informed her that a death certificate would be ready for her soon. But it seems Shipman made two mistakes here: the first being the way in which he left Grimshaw's body, it seemed relaxed, as if she had just fallen asleep (the effect morphine might have on a person), but he had suggested that she died of a stroke. Had another medical professional examined the body, they would have questioned this diagnosis, because people who die of a massive stroke usually have a seizures or muscles spasms, leaving their body and face contorted. Secondly, he had prepared the death certificate in advance; pre-empting that her body would be found on the same day, Shipman had filled in the date as the 14th, he then had to correct this to read the 15th. Computer experts later tracked fake entries in Grimshaw's records, implying she was at risk of having a stroke. He even dated some of the symptoms to a visit that was not registered in the practice's diary.

Elizabeth Mellor was the last victim to be exhumed. She had a previous history that would have appealed to Shipman – she had suffered a stroke in 1993. Since the stroke, she had become less active and was almost housebound. Her friend and downstairs neighbour, Joyce Harrison, spent a lot of time with her and would always listen out for movement in the flat; the sound of running water and the TV comforted her with the knowledge that Elizabeth was doing OK. On the 30th November 1994, Joyce remembers a knock at the door. It was the local pharmacist who had tried to deliver a prescription, but there was no answer. Shipman was using the people of the town like puppets. He had clearly arranged for the pharmacist to call, knowing there would be no answer and her caring neighbour would be alerted. Sure enough, Joyce let herself in and found Mellor dead in her chair. She immediately called Shipman – he would know what to do. Knowing her previous history, it was easy for Shipman to announce that she had died of a stroke. Joyce recalled to police that Shipman seemed gruff and agitated – he had even made reference to seeing her earlier that day, perhaps thinking Joyce would have spotted his visit. But he shouldn't have, because Joyce had not seen him visit. Perhaps if he hadn't given away this vital clue, then Joyce would not have passed this remark onto police and the death would not have seemed so suspicious. For so long, Shipman had done and said whatever he wanted with no one ever questioning him. He used his position in the community to sway people's thinking and convince them of a cause of death. He was so arrogant that he never thought people would later question what he said and that every throwaway comment would be remembered and used against him.

Of course, for the police, there were more than twelve bodies that raised cause for concern. They could have picked from fifty or sixty cases dating back years and years. However, there comes a point when the bodies taken for forensic analysis would provide enough evidence to show a distinct pattern of killing. It is more than likely that if they were to dig up every one of Shipman's buried victims, they would find morphine in their tissue. But for what purpose? The police now had enough evidence to charge Shipman with mass murder, enough that, if convicted he would never be a free man again. The digging up of any more bodies would cause a media circus, not to mention the distress and disruption it would bring to the community of Hyde and the relatives of the interred. Although the way in which Shipman had killed his victims was clean and peaceful – the way in his victims were examined was quite the opposite. The sight of regular exhumations was gruesome and shocking; it brought back memories of the deceased and there was an outpouring of sympathy for the relatives and then for the wider community in general. The people of Hyde were suffering the indignity of their loved ones' bodies being dragged out of the earth, all because of one doctor they welcomed in and trusted with their lives.

Each exhumed body required a forensic test, if not two. Two, because Shipman's defence also needed to examine the body. In the case of Kathleen Grundy, they were allowed to carry out their own pathology tests, but for the rest, the pathologist acting on behalf of the defence simply stood in on the examination carried out by John Rutherford – the pathologist used by the police. Carrying out a criminal pathology examination is time consuming, but once they had found Kathleen Grundy's death to be the result of excessive morphine in her body, they knew what to look for. A thorough examination was carried out on each victim, but they all came back with the same cause of death – a lethal dose of morphine.

Morphine is an opiate and Shipman's derivative of choice was diamorphine, which is, effectively, heroin. Diamorphine is like a double-strength dose of morphine and it acts faster and more aggressively in the body. It is commonly used as a painkiller, but also has other beneficial side-effects such as leaving a patient feeling relaxed. It isn't a euphoric drug, but it would leave you in a happy, blissful state. It is also addictive and can cause breathing problems, which is why Shipman was almost caught out a few times when using this drug with patients that he knew suffered from illnesses that affected breathing, such as asthma or bronchitis.

Morphine was not the most foolproof choice of drug for Shipman to use. It remained in the tissue after death, something that would later lead to a strong case against him in court; it also needs to be administered in the correct dosages to work; and it is a controlled substance – meaning Shipman was breaking the law just by carrying it around with him. He would have been better off using a less detectable substance, such as insulin. Insulin would be metabolized by the body and it would be impossible to determine a cause of death, unless a post-mortem was carried out and a single needle mark was noted.

So why morphine? Looking back to Shipman's early life and career, it is clear to see that he developed an obsession with opiates from the time of his mother's death. His mother was suffering from cancer and was regularly medicated with morphine; it is perhaps even possible that she was aided in her death by her GP administering one final, lethal dose. Shipman then began to experiment with pethidine, both in medical school, throughout his years as a junior doctor and until he was found out in Todmorden. He had developed a system for acquiring opiates that was tried and tested and he was familiar with the way the drug worked. He had also got away with so many murders in this way, that he probably did not consider it important that he was leaving evidence behind.

Shipman must have thought that he had got away with most crimes, because the majority of his victims were cremated. Many witnesses even remember him speaking about cremation and offering to supply cremation forms as soon as he had pronounced the death. He played on relatives during their most vulnerable moments, manipulating them into proceeding in the way that would best suit him. But he was wrong; the police were able to piece together enough circumstantial evidence to charge Shipman with the murders of six further victims that had been cremated. This was huge for the police, because, if proven in court, that Shipman had committed these murders also, then the same MO could be traced back and attributed to hundreds more deaths that they were earmarking as suspicious.

The police had never considered that there would ever be enough evidence to convict a person of murder without a body. However, statements from friends and relatives, combined with proof of forged medical records was enough. On its own, each case may not have stood up in court – but a clear pattern, the same story told over and over again and the obvious attempts to cover his tracks produced a bigger picture. Furthermore, Shipman had not realized that telephone records could also be traced; lies he had told about being called to a patients house, or claiming to call for an ambulance, began to unravel.

The first cremation death to be investigated was the case of Norah Nuttall. Norah was a large woman but was on the path to a healthier life, having lost eight stone in weight. She had seen Shipman at his open surgery on 26th January 1998; Shipman was such a popular doctor that she had queued for over two hours just to see him. He sent her away with some cough medicine and told her to stay at home. Later that day, Shipman visited her home and injected her with a lethal dose of diamorphine, but he was disturbed on his way out and Nuttall's son discovered Shipman at the front door. Shipman

Friends and relatives of the victims of Harold Shipman gather together for a special service of prayer. Hundreds attended St George's Church in Hyde, Greater Manchester for the ecumenical service, 1st February 2000.

Health Secretary Alan Milburn delivers a statement to the House of Commons in London, following the sentencing of Dr Harold Shipman for the murder of 15 of his patients, 1st February 2000.

The family of Bertha Moss share a quiet moment after a prayer service held for the victims of Harold Shipman. The death of Bertha Moss was investigated as a result of Shipman's conviction for the murder of 15 patients, 1st February 2000.

Dr Aneez Esmail, Lord Laming, and Professor Hazel Genn, three members of the panel who were overseeing the inquiry into serial killer Harold Shipman, 10th March 2000.

Families of victims of Dr Harold Shipman arrive at the High Court in London, beginning their legal battle for the independent inquiry into the deaths to be held in public, 27th June 2000.

Jane Gaskell, George Hurst, Brenda Hurst, Ann Whelan and Helen Blackwell, relatives of the victims of Harold Shipman, attend a judicial review of the case, outside London's High Court, 20th July 2000.

Danny Mellor, son of Shipman victim Winifred Mellor, following a judicial review of the case at London's High Court. Families of the victims won their High Court battle for an open inquiry into how their loved ones came to die, 20th July 2000.

Dr Richard Baker, University of Leicester professor, presents his findings in a report on convicted murderer Dr Harold Shipman during a news conference at the Department of Health in London, 5th January 2001.

Jane Ashton Jibbert, representative of the relatives of the victims of serial killer Harold Shipman, arrives at Manchester Town Hall for the start of the Shipman Inquiry, 20th June 2001.

General view of the chamber inside Manchester Town Hall that was used for the Shipman Inquiry, which began 20th June 2001.

Elaine Oswald arrives to give evidence at the Harold Shipman Inquiry, 9th November 2001. Oswald is believed to have been the intended first murder victim of Dr. Harold Shipman.

Suzanne Brock, granddaughter of one of Harold Shipman's victims, Edith Brock, 4th July 2002.

Peter Wagstaff, son of one of Harold Shipman's victims, Laura Wagstaff, 14th July 2003.

Dame Janet Smith delivers her second and third reports into the Harold Shipman Inquiry at Manchester Town Hall, 14th July 2003.

Manchester coroner John Pollard, pictured outside Manchester Town Hall where the second and third reports into The Harold Shipman Inquiry were being delivered, 14th July 2003.

improvised, saying that she was unwell and that he had called for an ambulance. Nuttall's son found this hard to believe, because he had been talking to her on the phone only an hour before. Her son went over to her and found that she was cold and could not be woken up. Shipman coolly announced that she had died and then pretended to call and cancel the ambulance. When the police heard her son's account of the death, some things did not add up: if she had only just died, why didn't Shipman attempt to resuscitate her? Why was he there at all? He had told her son that he'd received a call to visit, but there was no record of such a call. There was also no record of Shipman's supposed call to the ambulance service. When they looked into his computerised medical records, they discovered falsified entries claiming Nuttall was suffering from bronchitis, which coupled with her heart disease and high blood pressure put her at risk of a heart attack. At first glance, Nuttall's death was consistent with her medical records, had he not embellished further, he may have got away with that one, too.

When the Crown Prosecution Service accepted this charge against Shipman, the police had turned a huge corner in their investigations. In the exhumed bodies of older victims, there was not enough physical evidence to support a case for murder, but the case of Norah Nuttall set a new precedent for charging Shipman without physical evidence from the victim's body. The police were now able to proceed with enquiries into five more of Shipman's cremated victims. The next was Marie West. Her case dated back the furthest – to 1995.

Marie West was old and frail, but was certainly not near to death. She was visited regularly by Shipman to treat pains in her legs and hips. Shipman would regularly bring pain medication. When Shipman visited for the last time, Marie West was not alone. Her friend Maria

Hadfield was visiting, but had disappeared into the kitchen, choosing to give her friend some privacy whilst Shipman examined her. After a while she returned to the living room and found Shipman with Marie. Shipman had expected to be alone and wasn't prepared to see Mrs Hadfield. He made up a story of Marie collapsing on him and then announced that she had died – he did not bother to resuscitate. There were more inconsistencies with this case: Shipman noted the cause of death as stroke, which would not have happened silently. Mrs Hadfield remembered it being eerily quiet and returned from the kitchen because she thought the doctor had gone. Shipman also told Marie West's son a different account of events, saying he had left her alone while he went back to his car and that he had taken her blood pressure, however, there was no record of this. It is also unlikely that in the case of a sudden death like that, Shipman wouldn't have called for an ambulance or made an attempt to save her life. His acceptance of such a sudden death was shocking in itself.

There is evidence to show that Shipman orchestrated his next victim's death in advance. Lizzie Adams, aged seventy-seven, was allergic to penicillin, but Shipman had prescribed it to her. Now all he had to do was sit back and wait for her call. A house call was arranged and Shipman set off. But, once again, he hadn't anticipated Lizzie's friend, Bill, calling round. This seems to be a common pattern with Shipman. Perhaps in his own personal life, he had no friends or family that would just call by to check up – so this would have been an alien concept to him. Just like with Norah Nuttall, Shipman thought on his feet and informed Bill that Lizzie was ill and an ambulance had been called. Bill went over to Lizzie but she was unresponsive. Shipman casually announced that she had died, again making no attempt to save her life. Being there at the time of death gave Shipman the authority to say whether a post-mortem would be needed and because no one ever suspected that he was responsible for killing their loved one, his medical opinion was never question.

He informed the family that Lizzie had died from pneumonia, although, had this been the case she would not have looked peaceful and would have been fighting for her life and for air, for some time. Shipman correctly assumed that most people would not know this and got away with marking it on the medical form. But his lies about calling an ambulance, yet again, came back to haunt him and when police checked phone records – there was no such call.

The next victim was Kathleen Wagstaff. Witnesses remember Shipman making an unsolicited visit and that she seemed surprised when he turned up. This later contradicted what he told her daughter-in-law, Angela, who he had confused for her daughter and accidentally informed her of Kathleen's death. Angela was visited by Shipman who told her that her mother had requested him to visit and that he'd found her dead. Shipman hadn't even bothered to get his facts straight, making an assumption based on surname; he approached the wrong person and informed her that her mother had died. He didn't even give a name, so it wasn't until Angela called her actual mother, Ann Royle, that she realized Shipman had made a mistake – he never even apologised. Meanwhile Kathleen Wagstaff was dying. Shipman told her neighbour that she had died and he had tried to call an ambulance but it was too late. He also said that Wagstaff had asked him to make a visit. Both of these statements were proved to be lies when phone records were later cross-referenced against Shipman's account of the event. Shipman's next cremation victim to come to light was Pamela Hillier. Another so-called stroke victim, she died on 9th February 1998 and on that same day, Shipman logged six false entries into her medical records. Hillier was fit and active until she suffered a minor fall and came to visit Shipman at his surgery a few times. This seemed to be a repeating pattern amongst his victims. He would become familiar with them after a few visits. This was enough for them to become targets and he would later visit their home, on a pretext of a follow-up, and kill them. The most common excuses he used were that he had come to take blood, come to deliver medicine, or come to check up following a visit to the surgery. The pretext for Shipman's visit on the day of her death is not confirmed, although thought to be under the guise of delivering medication. Shipman put the cause of death as 'stroke', altered her medical records to show a history of high blood pressure, and broke the news to her family. However, the family were shocked and when Shipman said there would be no need for a post-mortem, they disagreed. A post-mortem would have revealed that she died of an overdose and that no stroke took place. Shipman would have to explain why he gave her so much morphine and why he was carrying it without a prescription in the first place. He came so close to being found out, but managed to convince the family that a post-mortem would be distressing and pointless, that because he knew her medical history he was best placed to determine the cause of death.

Shipman was becoming more brazen and his last cremation victim (for which he was convicted) was a bigger challenge. Maureen Ward was a young victim at fifty-eight, but had suffered from cancer in the past. She was living in a warden-controlled block of flats. On the day of her death, 18th February 1998, Shipman had convinced her to leave her flat unlocked so that he could pay a visit. Not long after he arrived, he buzzed through to the warden, informing her of Maureen's death and asking her to attend the scene. The warden was shocked, but Shipman had already premeditated the cause of death and already tampered with her medical files. He told the warden that Maureen had a brain tumour and it would have caused her to pass out and die. This was not a particularly plausible story, but Shipman had a certain air of authority that, quite obviously, got him far. He put down the cause of death as cancer in both the brain and the breast, despite giving her the all-clear for breast cancer in earlier, correct, medical notes. Shipman added to his lies when he gave a completely different account of events to his receptionist. He had such a low opinion of auxiliary staff, he probably thought he could tell her anything and her word against his would never stand up if questioned. He told the receptionist that he had been driving by and noticed an ambulance and went to investigate. He also stated on the death certificate that the warden had found the body, which was not true.

Shipman's lies would soon catch up with him. By now, police had enough evidence to bring forward a case to the Crown Prosecution Service.

Chapter 12

The Trial

The Trial

Shipman's trial lasted nearly four months. He was charged with fifteen separate murder counts and one count of forgery. The jury heard from hundreds of witnesses and family members, but in a revealing letter written to friends back in Hyde, Shipman showed what he really thought of himself, saying, "The big star has yet to come (me)."

It took a year for detectives to compile all of their evidence against Shipman. During that time, he was remanded in custody at Strangeways prison in Manchester. They had investigated so many suspicious deaths, yet families were still coming forward with stories of how Shipman had treated their loved ones in their final hours. Their list of potential victims had risen from one to three, to fifteen, to sixty and was now edging towards the hundreds. It was clear that Shipman had systematically killed hundreds of his patients, but it would be impossible to bring that number of victims to court.

It was decided fifteen cases would be brought to court – nine of victims that had been exhumed (forensic evidence was too weak in the cases of the older victims) and six that had been cremated. The six cremated victims were important because if guilt could be proved through circumstantial evidence alone, then Shipman's proven MO could then be extended to the other deaths and, although they wouldn't be tried in court, there would be precedent to state that he had killed many more. The reason to limit the victim count to fifteen was also due to the limitations of the court system and the toll it would take on the jury. To go through fifteen cases worth of evidence would be time-consuming and a huge amount of information for the jury to take in. Greater numbers would risk leaving the prosecution open to attack if they were to leave gaps in explanations of findings and it would be harder for the jury to focus on details that proved, beyond doubt, that Shipman had killed these women.

Shipman's trial began at Preston Crown Court on 5th October 1999. He was to face fifteen charges of murder and one charge of forgery. The names of the victims were revealed as: Kathleen Grundy, Winifred Mellor, Joan Melia, Bianka Pomfret, Marie Quinn, Ivy Lomas, Jean Lilley, Irene Turner, Muriel Grimshaw, Kathleen Wagstaff, Norah Nuttall, Maureen Ward, Pamela Hillier, Marie West and Elizabeth Adams.

The trial was a media circus – the press had latched onto the story of 'doctor death' and there was a constant scrum of paparazzi waiting to get a glimpse of Shipman as he arrived in the prisoner transportation van. Shipman's trial was unprecedented in its enormity and there were daily reports from news crews who had set up camp outside the courthouse.

Every day of the trial, Primrose would attend. Sometimes she had support from her children and, other times, from members of the local community. The public gallery would be split between those who supported Shipman and relatives of the deceased who were seeking justice.

Shipman had lost weight and aged dramatically during the year he was remanded in custody. Some observers from the gallery, who knew him before the trial, remarked on his appearance and that he seemed a shadow of his former self. Some sympathized, still believing he was caught up in a bogus witch-hunt. However he may have looked, he still had the same callous and superior attitude and many witnesses report him trying to intimidate them and stare them down whilst they were on the stand.

Shipman's defence was initially to try to get the whole thing thrown out of court. His barrister, Nicola Davies QC, argued that the whole case had been turned into a media circus. Exaggerations by the police and sensationalist stories would have swayed the jury into believing media reports rather than the facts presented in court. She wanted the trial to be split into smaller cases so that the case of Kathleen Grundy and her forged will was tried first, then the exhumations, followed by the cremations. She also tried to have evidence withheld, particularly regarding Shipman's stockpile of morphine and his methods to acquire on the grounds that the evidence related to cases that were not being tried in court. However, the judge denied these requests and the case went on.

There were many witnesses called to give evidence and speak about their deceased relative in the days and moments prior to death. Many found it difficult and had forgotten details – it was hard for grieving families to have to go through the tragedy again and in front of such a large audience. Many found it intimidating and distressing. All the while Shipman sat next to his barrister and fastidiously made notes. At this point, it seems he did not believe that he would be found guilty. He still thought that his word as their GP would be enough and that by denying everything and not saying a word – they couldn't prove that he had done it. But the evidence spoke for itself.

Witness after witness reported that their mother, or aunt or friend, had been in fine health just days before their death. One sudden death might not seem shocking, but so many in a row, all with Shipman present, all being discovered in the same way, with all the exhumed bodies containing large quantities of morphine, it didn't matter what Shipman had to say for himself. So, as the trial went on, he became less and less active; he wrote less and he conferred with his barristers less. It seems he just sat and let the proceedings happen around him, detaching himself emotionally – just like he had done when his mother had died.

The judge at the trial was Thanyne Forbes, he was sixty-one at the time and was experienced in high profile court cases. He was renowned for being fair and meticulously analysing the evidence. It was well known that none of his convictions had even been appealed successfully. Seven men and five women had been selected from a potential sixty jurors. Their first day set the tone for what was to come. This was one of the most serious and responsible cases a juror would ever have to sit on and it started with a grueling eight-hour long summary of the charges against Shipman.

The prosecution's opening line, however, was its strongest by laying out the cold, hard facts:

"None of them were prescribed morphine or diamorphine; all of them died unexpectedly; all of them had seen Dr Shipman on the day of their death; none of the deceased were terminally ill so euthanasia, or mercy killing, is out of the question. The defendant killed because he enjoyed it. He revelled in the ultimate power of controlling life and death, and repeated it so often that he must have found the drama of taking a life to his taste."

With a prosecution case as strong as this, and compared to the defence's opening statement that claimed the media sensationalism made the trial 'unfair', it was clear that Shipman had a tough battle ahead of him. But Shipman's arrogance had not faded that much and in a letter to a friend he revealed just what he thought of himself, saying, "The big star has yet to come (me)."

The first witness to the stand was Angela Woodruff, the woman who had uncovered Shipman for who he was, who had proved that he had forged her mother's will – she was Kathleen Grundy's daughter. Angela was followed by a trail of elderly friends and relatives and then younger relatives, angry and bitter at the premature loss of a loved one. The witnesses were not easily put off and Shipman's main defence tactic was to suggest that the elderly witnesses were confused and couldn't remember correctly. This tactic lost Shipman sympathy and his support began to dwindle.

The prosecution case lasted twenty-five days and included reports from the forensic pathologist, John Rutherford. Rutherford was able to confirm his findings from all nine of the cases where a body was exhumed. In each case Rutherford could find no other likely cause of death other than a lethal overdose of morphine, due to the substantial amount of morphine still found in their body tissue.

Experts on drugs and their effects were brought in to educate the jury on the effects of morphine. How much would be needed to kill and what the general effects of the drug were. They realized that for each victim to have willingly overdosed from morphine, then they would have had to stockpile over-the-counter versions of the drug for months. For example, they would have needed hundreds of codeine tablets or would have had to drink a litre plus of kaolin and morphine solution (something used for an upset stomach). There was no evidence of any of the over-the-counter medications found at any of the victims' houses.

The lesson on morphine was then backed up with evidence of how Shipman acquired such large quantities; there were statements from witnesses who had been supposedly prescribed large quantities of the drug claiming to have never taken it in their life. Witness after witness took the stand and told the court that they had never been treated with morphine, and were shocked to learn that their medical records showed prescriptions for it. Shipman had used his place in the community and his respected position as a doctor to dispense morphine from the local pharmacy, in his patient's names, and had never been stopped.

The defence began their case on 25th November 1999 and Shipman took to the stand the same day. He was allowed to build up a picture of himself, talk about his early career and the day-to-day activities in his practice. The defence were trying to show a different side to Shipman, not the side of a callous serial killer that had been depicted by the press.

The first case put to Shipman was that of Kathleen Grundy. His defence was based on his assumption that she was addicted to codeine or morphine (something that would also explain away the morphine in her system). But Shipman's defence was flawed because police could prove that he had falsified those records to say that in the first place. He claimed that she was old and frail and had approached him to witness her will. When he was asked outright, "Did you kill Kathleen Grundy?" His answer was a vehement, "No." Shipman was asked this question about the fourteen other victims, and each time he would answer the same, "No."

Shipman went on for days, answering questions about each victim. The only thing he admitted was backdating his computer records.

He claimed that this was just simple admin, bringing his notes in line from when the patient had first noticed symptoms. This goes against the meticulous and efficient image he had painted for himself as a family doctor, who was always on top of his other patient's conditions and always got the best treatment for them. He claimed the back-dating happened in other cases because the patient hadn't told him of any symptoms until the day they died. It must have been hard for his defence to believe that story.

When asked why he did not try to resuscitate the women involved, he said it was because he thought that their lives would have been impaired if they had lived, that the oxygen deprivation to their brain would have left them in a vegetative state. This contradicts most cases where they died in his presence; had he revived them immediately, then they would have been fine. Other reasons were even more dubious: because they would end up in a nursing home, or because they might suffer a loss of personality. All this did was reveal Shipman's negligence and arrogance that he believed it was up to him to determine whether they were better off dead. The most preposterous reason was the case of Ivy Lomas, who died at his surgery. He said he did not ask for help because he didn't want to disrupt the surgery. He claimed to have performed CPR on Mrs Lomas, but this contradicts the receptionist's story, who says he saw three patients whilst she was supposedly dying.

Shipman's defence was based around the fact that nobody could prove that he injected the victims. But his problem was that witness accounts of events contradicted his own, as did the stories he'd told different family members. His lies were catching up with him and his only defence was that he was telling the truth and the other people were confused, or out to get him.

Shipman chose not to offer an explanation as to why there was so much morphine consistently found in all of the exhumed bodies. He was backed into a corner with the case of Ivy Lomas and was forced to admit that, due to the high morphine levels, she would have died within minutes. How then could he deny administering the drug when she had been in his surgery for at least half an hour prior to her death? He did not admit to administering the drug, but admitted that she was never alone and wouldn't have gained access to it without his knowledge. By logical conclusion, the prosecution put it to Shipman that he must be guilty. Shipman replied saying, "That's what you're saying and I disagree with it strongly. I didn't administer anything to this lady and I have no idea how it got into her body." For such a caring and conscientious GP, that answer was simply not good enough.

Shipman's defence was severely lacking – they had no comeback for the pathology results on the exhumed bodies, despite a forensic pathologist for the defence being present at all examinations. They had no expert witnesses bar one person who spoke about the fingerprints on Grundy's will. The fact that Shipman's print was on the will was damning in itself, there was no way they could get around this fact and an expert fingerprint analyst did not help matters. His defence was quite simply, "I didn't do it."

The prosecution summed up their case after all the evidence had been reviewed and all the witnesses cross-examined.

"Not once in all these cases did you call an ambulance. Not once did you admit any patient to hospital. Not once did you permit a post-mortem. The simple explanation for all the evidence in this case is your guilt."

The jury was adjourned on 13th December 1999 and, after a break for Christmas, they returned on 5th January 2000. The prosecution began their summary by reminding the jury of the 100 plus witnesses and experts that they had listened to. They focused on Shipman's diabolical abuse of trust within the community of Hyde. Under the guise of caring for his patients, he had actually ended their lives. He had abused their trust and his position within the community to cover his tracks by manipulating grieving families into accepting his explanations for death and forcing through cremation forms and death certificates to save his own skin. He had knowingly falsified records, which proved his was a calculating killer, some he had even embellished prior to a kill. In summary, he was a cold and heartless killer who had duped a community into trusting them with their lives.

The defence then presented their summary of events. Nicola Davies played on Shipman's image as a respected and trusted doctor in the community and referred to those who still believed in his innocence as proof of this. She claimed he was the victim of a witch-hunt, that Shipman was being punished for going above and beyond the call of duty. She claimed that his inaccuracies in the records were because he devoted so much time to caring for his patients and that he was truly saddened that people would think so ill of him. In defence of his aloof and cold demeanour at the scene of a death, she explained again that this was simply down to his professionalism and competence as a doctor. She claimed he could not have forged Grundy's will, because of the 'crude and clumsy' way in which it was written – this would have been impossible for such an intelligent man. Despite not calling a toxicologist expert, Davies herself attempted to debunk the forensic reports, claiming that the evidence could not be trusted due to the state of decomposition. The judge then gave his summary, reiterating the serious nature of the charges. He reminded the jurors that they should not be swayed by emotional testimonies or sensationalism in the media and that they must consider the facts dispassionately. He also reminded them that each charge was a stand-alone case and they must come to a decision on each individual case. The jury retired to give their verdict on 24th January 2000. After five hours of discussion on the first day, they were sent home. It took six further days for them to reach decisions on each individual case; on 31st January 2000, the jury returned to court with their verdicts. The nominated foreman of the jury stood up and when asked by the judge, stated that all verdicts had been a unanimous decision. When asked how they found the defendant, the answer came back the same for each charge, "Guilty." Shipman showed no emotion.

The judge passed sentence immediately and told Shipman, "You murdered each and every one of your victims by a calculated and cold-blooded perversion of your medical skills for your own evil and wicked purposes. You took advantage of and grossly abused their trust. You were, after all, each victim's doctor. I have little doubt that each of your victims smiled and thanked you as she submitted to your deadly ministrations."

The judge passed fifteen consecutive life sentences as well as a four-year sentence for forgery. Unlike most cases of life imprisonment, where the judge sends a recommendation of time to the home secretary, in this particular case, Mr Justice Forbes recommended that life meant life. He recommended that Shipman spend the remainder of his days behind bars with no possibility for parole.

After Shipman was led away, the judge went on to pay an emotional tribute to the relatives and witnesses who had shown dignity and restraint throughout the proceedings. He thanked them for their contributions and hoped that the verdict would at least go some way to achieving peace for the victims. He also thanked the police and the jurors, making it known what a huge ordeal and undertaking it had been for them. The court was dismissed and Shipman was whisked away to spend the rest of his life in jail. The first stop was Strangeways.

Chapter 13

Why?

Why?

> *Jail was Shipman's final destination. He committed suicide, by hanging himself in his cell. Secret documents have since revealed that prison guards believed that he would continue killing inside prison. He reportedly threatened one inmate, saying, "Remember I am a doctor, I know where to cut you." Prison officers even gave orders that he should be kept away from elderly inmates, due to his history.*

The question that springs to most people's minds when they hear about Harold Shipman is why? What possessed him to take so many lives? Was it a sick power game? Was he addicted to killing? Was it pathology, like a bizarre obsessive-compulsive ritual that he couldn't stop? Maybe he got a buzz from taking a life? Maybe he thought he was helping them, by putting them out of their misery? The truth is, no one will ever know for sure, because he took the answer to the grave with him. The only answer that comes remotely close to answering this question is what he told the courts when he was presented with the cases against him, "I treated each patient as was appropriate to their condition at the time."

Some serial killers are actually copycat killers, inspired by the murders of earlier serial killers. For example, the Japanese killer who copied the 'Zodiac' killer that operated twenty years previously. The 'Zodiac' killer stalked his victims and then shot them, leaving behind cryptic clues for the police. The original 'Zodiac' was never caught, but Eddie Seda was caught out copying the kills after leaving behind fingerprints at a crime scene. Even Britain's most famous serial killer, Jack the Ripper had a copycat – Derek Brown killed prostitutes in the Whitechapel area of London in 2008, almost 120 years after the original Jack the Ripper crimes. Could Shipman have been copying someone else's MO?

In 1957, British general practitioner, Dr John Bodkin Adams, was tried, and later acquitted, for the murder of one of his patients. Adams is little-known to the world today, but may have been somebody Shipman was aware of and who Shipman may have even studied during his time at medical school. Although Adams was never found guilty of murder, over 150 of his patients died in suspicious circumstances over a period of just ten years. What's more, many of his patients left him money in their wills, or items of jewellery – sound familiar?

One of Adams' notable patients was Edith Morrell. She had suffered from a stroke and Adams continued to visit her and administer pain medication. Looking back at medical records, it seems he gradually increased the doses of morphine and then diamorphine until Morrell was addicted. He used the power of opiate addiction to make her sign things over to him in her will. She eventually died two and half years after her initial stroke. Adams filled in her cremation form stating he had no pecuniary interest (i.e. he would not benefit from her death in any way) and recommended that there was no need for a post-mortem.

Adams' next suspected victim was Gertrude Hullett. Hullett suffered from depression following her husband's death and Adams had prescribed her barbiturates. Six days prior to her eventual death, Hullett gave Adams a cheque for £1,000. Two days later she slipped into a coma. Adams failed to mention her barbiturate use and instead suggested the cause of the coma was a cerebral haemorrhage, actively steering pathologists away from a toxicology test. Just like Shipman, he used his superiority to convince others of a certain idea. When Hullett eventually died, the post-mortem revealed a fatal does of sodium barbitone in her system. Had Adams killed her once he had got his money?

The ensuing court case was a precedent setter and, as such, did not go well. The defence concluded that any evidence against Adams was circumstantial and there was no proof that he had killed the women. In fact Adams himself was quoted as saying, "Murder? Can you prove it was murder? She was dying in any event."

It is likely that Adams was guilty, but the NHS was new at that time and a guilty verdict would have knocked public confidence. He was also a member of the ruling class and had friends in high places. It is likely that the case was interfered with at the highest level – something that would not happen to Shipman in much more modern and equal times. Adams may well have got away with murder, but could he still have been a role model for Shipman?

There are other famous 'Angel of Death' doctors that may have sparked an interest in Shipman. First off, Josef Mengele; Mengele was a Nazi doctor who operated in Auschwitz. He had an obsession with twins and had free reign to experiment on whomever he picked out at the concentration camp. He would perform cruel experiments and kill on a whim, all as part of an ongoing goal to cultivate a superior race. This was nothing like Shipman's MO, but it shows how the power dynamic between a doctor and patient can be taken to the extreme.

To think that someone going into the healing profession would choose to inflict pain and suffering is a juxtaposition, but there are many recorded cases of doctors doing just that and getting a thrill from the power they have over life and death. Dr Michael Swango, from Quincy, Illinois, was a modern-day Mengele and got away with killing many of his patients, even though people spoke out against him. Swango was a sociopath and got a buzz from witnessing deaths. He started off by trying to poison his colleagues and when later questioned by the FBI, he admitted that he did it just "to see what would happen".

Shipman was not the only doctor who had abused his power for evil rather than good. Adams, and other doctors who killed, may or may not have been a role model for Shipman, but what were the other influences? What drives a person to take the life of another human being?

Early Trauma:

The death of his mother had a profound effect on Shipman. During his mother's illness and deterioration, it would have been Shipman that predominantly cared for her. Harold saw first-hand the positive effects of morphine; he would have witnessed the whole procedure from the doctor preparing the syringe to the injection and the ensuing relief and respite that it gave his mother. It is not hard for criminologists to make the link between Shipman's chosen method for killing his patients and his early experiences with his dying mother; he would even choose to administer his lethal doses of morphine in the afternoon – consistent with his mother's experiences. His mother's death would have ignited mixed emotions inside the young and emotionally repressed Harold Shipman. To lose his mother would have been devastating, particularly at such a young age. However, the relief and release that would have followed that final dose of morphine would have also instilled a peace inside him that she was no longer in pain. And perhaps feeling relief at her death would have then led to feelings of anguish and perhaps even guilt. Conceivably, this inner turmoil may have led Shipman to seek out the peace he must have felt witnessing the pain leave his mother; perhaps his subsequent kills were a way to reconnect to that moment, to find that moment of peace once again?

Euphoria:

There is one theory that links the feeling of euphoria to death. When Shipman's mother died, Shipman went off on a long run for hours on end. The relief of his mum's passing combined with the release of endorphins through exercise permanently linked the feeling of euphoria with the death. A feeling he would try to find again and again by killing old ladies in the same way his mother had died.

Heroism:

Being a doctor makes you a hero. Shipman was well-known for being an arrogant man with an over-inflated ego and he would have needed a way to continually keep his ego inflated. By turning patients, who were seemingly fine, into medical emergencies, it meant that he could take the lead role over and over again. There is a common pattern in most of Shipman's cases where he is either at the scene when the patient dies, or is called by the family. This placed him in the starring role, the go-to person that everyone needed. Even if the patient died, it didn't matter, because the attention was deflected to Shipman and he became the saviour, the person who can denote cause of death, who knows what to do in the situation and who to call next.
He became a needed and respected member of the community.

Experimentation:

People become doctors because they are naturally curious about the human body. Shipman displayed clear signs of experimentation with drugs throughout his early years of medical school and also as a junior doctor. He took drugs himself and eventually became addicted. Could it be that the killings were simply an escalation of experiments into the effects of opiates on a human being? There is evidence he experimented with pethidine doses on two separate patients whilst he was a doctor in Pontefract. If one experiment went too far and he accidentally killed a person, it could have sparked a new interest – how to kill effectively with opiates. His death toll could have simply been the by-product of morbid experiments that purely served his own curiosity.

Power and Ego:

It is common knowledge that Shipman was an arrogant man. Many commented on his over-inflated ego. There are many accounts of his talking down to auxiliary staff members, making them feel stupid, no doubt to make himself feel more superior. Was the killing just an extension of this? His mother had raised him as the favoured child and built up a strong sense of self-importance in him. Throughout his life he protected himself from rejection, perhaps even with his choice of spouse, and this led to an increasingly inflated ego. Could the killings be an extension of his ego, a way for him to feel in control and to feel superior. He had ultimate control over his patient's lives and this would have made him feel powerful. Knowing he could play the authorities just by using his standing as a doctor would have bolstered him further. The act of getting away with murder and getting his inaccurate death certificate to be accepted without question would have fed into Shipman's self-importance and belief that he was above question and above the law.

Psychopathy:

From an early age, Shipman showed signs of psychopathy. Following his mother's death, his emotional blankness in the face of such tragedy was possibly more shocking than the tragedy itself. No witnesses ever saw him shed a tear or even look sad. Instead he remained stoic and just 'got on with things'. This kind of emotional distancing could be attributed to many things, perhaps it was just his way of dealing with grief, perhaps he had undiagnosed tendencies towards autism or Asperger's syndrome, or more worryingly – it could point to psychopathy; a psychopath being someone who is incapable, or has a diminished sense, of empathy and remorse. Later in life he would show the same blankness at the news of his father's death. In fact, the only death he appears to have been affected by was the death of a baby that was due to his medical negligence after he gave the pregnant mother too much pethidine. Was he upset about the death, or was just angry that he had got something wrong? Shipman hated being wrong and always had to be the best. Being able to kill indiscriminately for so long and never show the slightest bit of remorse has all the hallmark signs of a psychopath. Being a psychopath has its advantages in life, because you are not held up by emotion. Shipman's murders may have simply been an extension of paperwork. He needed his patient lists to be neat and tidy and his work life to be as smooth as possible. When he first worked in Pontefract, there is a pattern of elderly patients, likely to die soon, all dying around the same time. Could this have just been a way of Shipman getting them out of the way at the same time, so he wouldn't have to be called out later? In his later career, his kills may have been a way of keeping his patient list tidy. He only killed patients he was aware of medically, ones who visited the surgery often. Were they a nuisance that he got rid of in the most extreme way. A psychopath does not feel like a normal human being, so an extreme solution like this would not bother Shipman as it would other people.

Bloodlust:

For some, committing a violent death is as exciting as a sexual encounter. They want the heightened feeling that comes from the excitement of killing, or watching others react to a death. Whilst it is not always sexual, the feeling is like that of a sexual release and the need for another release will build up again, just like sexual frustration. Another 'Doctor of Death', Michael Swango, described a major fatal accident as his 'ultimate fantasy'; he also admitted how much he loved telling parents that their child was dead, the anticipation, he said, would give him an erection.

Addiction:

Did Shipman have an addictive personality? He showed, earlier in his life, that he developed a severe dependency to pethidine. Perhaps one addiction replaced another. Many serial killers get addicted to the act or the ritual of killing. It could be a case of bloodlust, or it could be a more psychological problem, an addiction that they have to satisfy. Shipman's pattern of escalation fits with the theory of addiction. Every year he worked as a GP, more and more patients died. But there are periods where he didn't kill. For example, when he was in rehab for his pethidine addiction, or after occasions where he was nearly found out – his killing stopped for a while. Also, whilst he was busy opening up his new practice, he did not kill anyone. After questions were raised about Kathleen Grundy's death, there were no more killings. Surely if he was so addicted that he had to kill over thirty people in one year, he would not have been able to just stop and go cold turkey.

Misplaced Compassion:

Shipman was in the habit of killing his elderly female, and sometimes male, patients. Could it be that this was an extreme version of euthanasia? Like John Bodkin Adams built up his patients' dependency on morphine or barbiturates to ease the passage, perhaps Shipman thought he was doing the same thing. He was ending the suffering of his poor, ailing patients. Shipman's mother suffered a long, drawn-out death from cancer and it is likely that she longed for death to come. Shipman would have witnessed this and felt powerless. He eventually saw the power his own GP had when he sent Shipman's mother into a morphine-induced coma and she peacefully passed away. Perhaps he had been playing out this scenario ever since, doing for others what he could not do for his own mother.

Inner Conflict:

In court, he displayed indifference to the suffering he had caused many families and contempt for the prosecution, which is indicative of sociopathy. However, according to Dr Chris Missen, head of forensic psychology at Anglia Polytechnic University, Shipman secretly hated himself. He had watched his mother die when he was seventeen, which he may have interpreted as rejection and abandonment and he may have lived his life feeling like he had disappointed her – something that, up until her death, he had always worked so hard not to do. His defence was based on the presumption that he had an impulse control problem, but in truth, he had been highly organised in the way he altered medical records and with the pretence with which he turned up to people's houses. He'd even forged Kathleen Grundy's will – a clear sign of premeditation. "What might have been perceived as a deep inner hypersensitivity," says Missen, "may have been no more than a swollen ego, in danger of imploding at the least pinprick." Shipman could not handle potential rejection from women the age his mother would have been, and it brought out his inner conflicts. In order to not feel the abandonment and disappointment he felt from his dead mother, he killed patients to keep from killing himself.

Pathology:

It is harder to understand killings performed by a doctor, given the nature of their work. Like other serial killers, their murders are premeditated, but juxtaposed with the fact that they actually care for the majority of their patients, and kill a minority. Some criminologists believe it is a pathology and one that is easy to discover if you accidentally kill someone as a young doctor. Just as some serial killers have a hunger for violence and act out a repressed fantasy over and over again, doctors who kill feel a similar empowerment from the thrill of taking a life, either the end result or through the act of killing itself. A pathology is almost like an addiction, but it becomes a subconscious compulsion, a need to do something over and over again for no reason shared with the conscious part of the brain. Shipman could have been acting in a pathological way, separating his actions from his perception of sense, believing that what he was doing was perfectly normal and acceptable. This explains why killings stopped when he was made to stop and think or to cover up when people asked questions or got too close. His conscious self became aware and controlled his behaviour for a while.

Doubling:

There is a common theory amongst criminologists called doubling.

This is thought to be a way the brain deals with actions that jar against socially acceptable ideas of good and evil. A doctor who kills his patients is in constant psychological conflict. Robert Jay Lifton, a psychiatrist who has studied the effects of war and seeing traumatic deaths, believe that a person splits in two following a conflicting event, such as killing a person who you are supposed to be caring for. Lifton refers to doubling as way of bargaining for your soul, you have to sacrifice part of yourself to gain control over your outward-facing persona. This is not the same as schizophrenia or dissociative personality disorder; doubling is a conscious way of adapting. He can redistribute his sense of morality in order to accommodate the desire to kill, whilst retaining the other side that would never do such a thing. This explains how Shipman was so loved by the community. He was a genuinely good GP and helped many of his patients; he set up a charitable fund to provide equipment for people who were suffering. Yet that same man coldly and callously killed his patients in their home. Was the first person just an act, a way of covering up his crimes and bolstering his ego – or was he doubling himself in order to separate the part of him that needed to kill? The doubled self can act autonomously, but can still be connected to the prior self from which it came. That way, a doctor can view himself as a compassionate, humane person and still go out and kill. The killing self provides a means for the prior self to survive without guilt. However, there's always the danger that the killing self can take over and become dominant, as was the case with the Nazi doctors and as could have been the case with Shipman in the last three to four years of his career; during this time deaths were happening every week and he was becoming less approachable, more insular and condescending. Lifton believes that doctors are more naturally inclined to the phenomena of doubling because they are expected to have two 'selves' in everyday life. The real person and the medical persona; they also learn to separate emotion from examination and are expected to examine a dead body without compassion for the person that once inhabited it.

Whatever the reason or motives behind Shipman's crimes, they are still shocking and inexcusable. The fact that he was able to kill again and again without question, abusing the power and trust he had over a small community goes against values held dear in a civilised society. Shipman was eventually found out for the killer he was. Perhaps he had a dark obsession with serial killers and was inspired by other murderers he'd read about. Perhaps he was seduced by the power of being a doctor and influenced by his early experiences during his mother's fight with cancer. Perhaps his experiments went too far and he became addicted to the feeling of killing. Perhaps he got a sexual pleasure from the deaths and had a physical urge to satisfy it. Perhaps he was a psychopath and it was his way of tying up loose ends. Perhaps he was full of inner angst and feelings of abandonment following his mother's death and was projecting feelings of self-harm and suicide. Perhaps he saw himself as an 'Angel of Death', killing out of compassion in order to end suffering. The truth is, we will never know exactly what possessed Shipman to do what he did, but his reign of terror came to an abrupt end when he was finally jailed for the rest of his natural life.

Chapter 14

Jail

Jail

Apart from the 250 plus deaths he is now known to be responsible for, Shipman's most obvious legacy was the Shipman Inquiry and the reforms it made. The investigation took five years to complete and cost the UK taxpayer over £21 million. The inquiry uncovered major flaws in the system of registering deaths and concluded that Shipman had begun killing in 1971 in Pontefract, going on to take the lives of around 250 more victims over the next 27 years. The exact number of murders remains unknown.

Even being convicted of just those fifteen murders meant Shipman was the most prolific serial killer in the UK. Shipman received back-to-back life sentences and was led out of the court, into the police transportation van and back to Strangeways Prison in Manchester. But it was not over, there were many more families who thought, quite rightly, that Shipman had murdered their relative and there was a growing feeling that more needed to be done, that justice had not yet been served.

Shipman was taken to a special wing at Strangeways where he would be on twenty-four hour suicide watch. He was about to endure one of the loneliest periods of his life. He no longer had regular meetings with his legal team and Primrose's visits were restricted from one per day (which he was allowed when before proven guilty and just remanded in custody) to one visit per week. Primrose and the children often visited him, but the police, who had further questions, also visited him. They wanted to know about more deaths, they wanted to help provide answers for more and more relatives who were coming forward. But Shipman refused to cooperate. He claimed it was harassment. He was inundated with letters from the media and

Sisters Helen McConnell and Betty Clayton, relatives of one of Harold Shipman's victims, Bertha Moss, pictured outside Manchester Town Hall, 14th July 2003.

Danny Mellow, relative of Winifred Mellor who was killed by Dr Harold Shipman, pictured outside Manchester Town Hall during the Shipman Inquiry, 14th July 2003.

Dr Harold Shipman is pictured in this undated Greater Manchester Police file photo.

Police officers escort a van believed to contain the body of Harold Shipman from Wakefield Prison in Yorkshire, northern England, 13th January 2004.

Wakefield Prison, Yorkshire, where Harold Shipman was found hanging in his cell, 13th January 2004.

Sam Shipman, son of Dr Harold Shipman, arrives at his Mother's home following news of his father's suicide in prison, 13th January 2004.

The former surgery of Dr Harold Shipman is covered with graffiti reading 'Justice' in Hyde, Manchester, on the day that the killer hanged himself, 13th January 2004.

Flowers arrive at the home of Primrose Shipman, the widow of Dr Harold Shipman, in Walshford, North Yorkshire, on the day that the prison ombudsman began his independent inquiry into the death of Dr Shipman at Wakefield Prison, 14th January 2004.

Primrose Shipman, the widow of Dr Harold Shipman, leaves her home as the prison ombudsman began his independent inquiry into the death of Dr Shipman, 14th January 2004.

Peter Bennett and Rajesh Patel, two doctors accused of failing to notice 'extraordinary coincidences' surrounding the death of Harold Shipman's patients, 22nd November 2004.

Ann Alexander, the solicitor who represented the victims of Dr Harold Shipman, who was present as the Shipman Inquiry released its final report, 27th January 2005.

Pharmacist Ghislaine Brant arrives to attend a statutory meeting where she is due to answer questions relating to her professional issuing of drugs, including diamorphine, to the late serial killer, Dr Harold Shipman, 21st February 2005.

Pathologist Dr. Phillip Lumb, who carried out the post mortem on Harold Shipman, pictured at the inquest into Shipman's death, 11th April 2005.

A split rock engraved with the word tranquility in new Garden of Tranquility to commemorate those who died at the hands of mass murderer Dr Harold Shipman, 30th July 2005.

Dr Harold Shipman photographed in Hyde, Greater Manchester.

from relatives, but refused to answer any of them, holding out for a possible appeal case he might be able to bring before the courts. He still believed he could get away with it. He still wanted to control the situation.

Soon, Shipman was moved to Frankland prison in Durham. Whilst it is a maximum-security prison, it is considered a luxury compared to other prisons and is filled with prisoners who are deemed high risk, either to themselves or others. This meant that Shipman was monitored almost all the time, but he also had it easy. He had satellite television, he didn't have to wear a uniform, he was allowed to socialise with other inmates, exercise in the gym and work a prison job. It was like a retirement home for him.

Although Shipman was good at hiding his emotions, it was clear to staff and fellow inmates that he enjoyed to read about himself and almost revelled in the attention. When other inmates would ask him, "How did you do it?" He would tell them to read the newspapers. There were countless documentaries on TV that he would have been able to watch, including a dramatisation by ITV starring James Bolam as Harold Shipman. If Shipman was one of those serial killers that got a sick pleasure from the infamy his crimes brought he was being allowed to revel in it.

Meanwhile, Primrose had been left almost destitute. Their house had to be sold to pay for legal fees, and without his salary, she now had to seek help from the welfare system. She was practically homeless and had to stay with each of her sons for weeks at a time.

Shipman almost enjoyed life at Frankland Prison. He had problems with his eyes and chose to take a course in reading and writing braille. Just like his A-levels all those years ago, he actually failed his braille exam the first time around, but he tried again and managed to pass the second time. He earned money working with other prisoners on a Braille translation of Harry Potter and, despite his limitations with the English language, he was in charge of proof-reading their work. He was renowned for his poor grammar and even did badly in English exams at school. His grammatical mistakes let him down in the forgery of Kathleen Grundy's will, too. Shipman was still asserting himself as a superior intellect due to his career as a doctor, as it is unlikely he would have got that job through skill alone.

He did not give up flaunting his medical knowledge either. Around the prison he was a famous face and people knew he was a doctor. They would often ask him for advice or a second opinion. Shipman became so obstructive to medical staff at the prison because he contradicted their diagnoses and questioned their prescriptions that he had to be moved away from the exercise wing, which was where he would hold his unofficial surgeries. Shipman had found a new popularity amongst criminals. Just like he had been a popular member of the community in Hyde, he was even popular in prison, with people just as immoral as he was.

True to form, Shipman was well known for talking down to fellow inmates and prison guards – he obviously thought himself superior to those around him and his favourite insult was to call people stupid. But there was one thing Shipman hadn't counted on, and that was therapy. Just as he had done with the police, Shipman refused to talk about his crimes, or still even admit he had done anything wrong. The usual way to tempt prisoners into therapy is through parole and the possibility of release, but Shipman knew it was all or nothing. He was in jail for the rest of his life, unless he won an appeal – there was no incentive for him to go to therapy, in fact it could jeopardise any future case he might bring to court if he let slip that he might have murdered someone.

Shipman spent years working towards appealing his case.
He contacted hundreds of law firms in and around Manchester,
looking for someone to represent him, but, unsurprisingly, no one
wanted to get involved. Many of them were too busy, in fact, dealing
with compensation claims lodged by families affected by his murders.
Several times whilst he was working on his appeal, he was placed on
suicide watch. There was a growing fear that should the appeal
process not go in his favour, he would be tempted to take his own
life and there was more than one reason for this. One major reason
was that his ego would not have been able to handle the blow, the
final decision that would mean he had been found guilty and was
not leaving prison. But there was another reason: he might forfeit
his pension for good if he lost, but if he died, Primrose would be
able to draw his pension and be supported financially.

Frankland was like a holiday home for criminals and Shipman didn't
realise how lucky he was until his luck changed. Unfortunately,
playing doctor with the other inmates had attracted some attention
and whilst most appreciated his help, others found it funny and a
small minority found it quite distasteful – for obvious reasons. Stories
of him wheeling around elderly patients and being allowed to weigh
in on diagnoses reached the tabloids and it wasn't long before the
irony captured the public's imagination. But for the people of Hyde it
was raw and these stories upset and angered people whose lives had
been ruined by Shipman's malpractice. There was a public outcry and
Shipman's easy ride in the, so-called, luxury prison was about to be
over. Frankland's team and their methods came under fire and it was
decided that Shipman had to be moved.

Shipman might have pretended to fellow inmates, or to his family,
that the move to Wakefield was at his request, claiming it was so that
he could be closer to Primrose, but this was unlikely. Primrose had
moved back to her home town of Wetherby following the death of
her mother, Edna Oxtoby. Edna never liked Shipman and in her will,

she had completely bypassed Primrose and left her £200,000 estate to the grandchildren. This would have annoyed Shipman greatly. If Primrose had received the inheritance then she would have been able to use that money to fund his appeal. Primrose was still a devoted wife and continued to visit him every week – either believing he was innocent, or simply being so in love with him that she accepted his actions without question.

Wakefield was a horrible prison compared to Frankland. Wakefield prison is full of the dregs of society. Shipman would have come up against much more hostile cell mates and lunchtime companions. At Wakefield, a high percentage of the prison population are sex offenders and paedophiles – people who would usually be shunned or constantly attacked in a different prison. Sex offenders are the lowest of the low and often make for creepy prison companions. Wakefield was also a much stricter environment where prison officers ran a tight ship. Anybody who stepped out of line knew about it, and even more distressing for Shipman – he was only allowed two visits per month.

The prison routine had far fewer privileges and it meant a lot more time locked away in his cell. He would get three basic meals, some exercise time and the opportunity to take some basic education classes. He was also required to attend therapy sessions and these were enforced much more emphatically than at Frankland. The draconian staff at Wakefield Prison did not tolerate Shipman's condescending and superior attitude at all. And it wasn't just his attitude that got him into trouble with staff – Shipman refused to attended two separate therapy sessions; cognitive self-change and enhanced thinking groups required lifers to participate in order to earn points for early release, but Shipman did not have this incentive. So instead, they de-incentivised him by reducing his privileges, including his television. He was also locked in his cell for longer and his weekly wage was reduced by over 50%. There was no softly-softly approach here and Shipman was getting the treatment that many felt he deserved.

Shipman's son, Christopher, contacted more law firms on his behalf. Most law firms would run a mile, or make up an excuse as soon as they heard the name Shipman. It took him months of calls and visits, but eventually, he found one firm that was willing to take on Shipman's appeal and the files were sent over. The lawyer that took on his case was Di Stefano, a controversial barrister who has represented shady figures in the past, including Slobodan Milosevic, former President of Serbia accused of violating the customs of war. For Shipman, working towards an appeal and eventual acquittal was, now, all he lived for. That, and seeing his wife. Even though he never showed emotion and nobody knew much about their married life, he appeared to dote on her in prison. They would kiss and hold hands throughout her visits and it appeared that he really did miss her. Perhaps he wasn't a psychopath after all, or perhaps he was clinging onto the one person who still admired him. Every single other person who had once looked up to him and respected him so much had now become disillusioned and angry. Even worse, some looked down on him and considered him to be stupid – the ultimate slight in Shipman's opinion. Slowly his supporters had dwindled away in the face of mounting evidence and story after story printed in the media. A couple of people Shipman initially had correspondence with had since stopped writing, distancing themselves from him as his letters became more and more self-involved, depressing and delusional. His stories began to contradict themselves and it was clear to all involved that he was guilty of taking the lives of those fifteen women, if not more. Shipman was running out of support in Hyde.

The contents of his letters have since been released and exposed by the BBC. In one letter he said, "No one saw me do anything. As for stealing morphine off the terminally ill, again, no one saw me do it." This superiority was reminiscent of John Bodkin Adams' response when he was accused of murder, Adam said, "Murder? Can you prove it?" Shipman's whole appeal seemed to be based on the fact that nobody saw him do it. How could they prove that he was responsible if nobody ever saw him inject a patient? But, as we have already discovered, the evidence against him was damning. He could never explain why he falsified medical records, or why the exhumed bodies had such high levels of morphine in their tissue; he either denied it, or went silent when he had no answer.

During his time in prison, Shipman was taken to Halifax where he was questioned about suspicious deaths in Todmorden. For these interviews, he chose to turn his back to the interviewer and not say a single word.

Shipman was not faring well in his new prison regime. His whole life had been based on control. He loved being in control and had exercised control over his wife, his family and his patients everyday. He had played the people of Hyde like puppets, prompting people to check on their relatives, knowing full well they were dead and waiting to be found. He had no regard for the psychological impact finding a dead body might have on a person. He controlled their medical records, their prescriptions and, ultimately, their deaths. In prison he had no control whatsoever; he was told when to wake up, when to eat, when to exercise, when to wash, when to go to bed, and was even forced into therapy through deprivation of privileges. Shipman tried his best to exert control in prison by trying to bully staff the way he used to bully 'inferior' colleagues, but they were not intimidated by Shipman, who was now starting to look frail and weak. Even wearing a uniform would have diminished his power; back in Frankland, he didn't have to wear a uniform. Once he realized he had no control whatsoever, then everything that made him tick, the essence of

Harold Shipman, disappeared. Everything that made him self-important no longer existed – no wife to wait on him and agree with his every whim, no adoring patients, no waiting list to get into his surgery. Perhaps having the power over life and death was what he lived for? Without this power and control in his life, he was a shadow of his former self.

Psychologists at the prison needed to assess whether Shipman was at risk of suicide. When he was first taken to Strangeways, he was under twenty-four hour supervision and he had been on suicide watch several times before. It was becoming more and more obvious to Shipman that an appeal would be futile and he was running out of money to fund his expensive lawyers. Psychologists who looked back at Shipman's time in prison believed that the only thing Shipman now had control over was his own life. And to have that control, he needed to convince wardens that he would not commit suicide. He even agreed to attend group therapy sessions so that he could gain back his television privileges.

Shipman thought that he could fool prison psychologists and deliberately wrote about food in his letters. He knew his letters would be vetted and scanned for signs of suicide and he knew from his medical background that people who are severely depressed, show little to no interest in food. He had to keep up a façade of being interested and engaged in prison life in order to hide the fact that he wanted to die.

Shipman had managed to convince staff that he was at no risk until his status as 'high risk' was lowered and he was allowed more unsupervised time in his cell. On 13th January 2004 Shipman hanged himself from the bars of his cell window. He knew he had an hour's time gap in which to take his own life, as prison officers made checks every hour. The last check had been at 5am; but Shipman only needed a few minutes to take his own life. He had torn up his bed sheets to create a make-shift rope. Wearing only a T-shirt, boxer shorts and socks, he balanced himself on the heating pipe and wrapped himself in the curtains that his wife had sent from home for him and then jumped. No one knows if he died instantly, or if he slowly asphyxiated himself to death. A prison guard running regular check looked through the spy hole at 6.15am and saw his feet dangling beneath the curtain. He pulled him down and tried to resuscitate him (something Shipman had failed to do for so many of his own dying patients), but it was too late – Shipman was already dead.

A prison doctor was called, who declared that Shipman was officially dead at 8.10am. Only a few hours later, transport had been arranged and he was on his way to Sheffield for a post-mortem examination (something else most of his murdered patients never received).

Carole Peters was able to find excerpts from Shipman's diary dating back as far as 1998, from when he was first incarcerated. The excerpts show he was in constant conflict with himself, some days wanting to die, which can be seen in extracts that read:

"So depressed, there is no way I can carry on…"

"My wife and kids have to go on without me when it is the right time. Got to keep the façade in tact for the time being…"

"If I was dead, they'd stop being in limbo. I'm desperate, no one to talk about it who I can trust. Everyone will want to talk to the prison officers and then I'll be watched 24 hours a day and I don't want that."

But only weeks later, he seemed more positive and had regained control of his life.

"A new year…I'll have to lock down this overwhelming emotion."

The ultimate control for Shipman was never admitting to his crime.

If he died before his appeal made it to court, then there would always be a question mark over his guilt. Even up to his death people were donating money to fund his defence. It goes to show just how strong the influence of a doctor over his patients can be. Shipman had made such an impression to the people of Hyde that many still believed his innocence and that was something that Shipman needed to hold on to. In fact, to this day, there are still people who believe his innocence. Perhaps he timed his death so that he would go before he ran out of support entirely, before the courts found him irrefutably guilty.

Some believe the timing of his death was about control and never getting to a stage where everyone, including his wife, might believe he was guilty. His ego needed to believe that he was in control and that people still looked up to him. But others believe that there was a different reason: Primrose. Whilst he remained alive, Shipman could not provide for his wife and she had gone from living a comfortable life as part of a close-knit community, to a transient bag lady sleeping in her son's spare bedroom. She even had to claim money from the welfare system in order to survive. Because of his criminal conviction and jail sentence, Shipman had forfeited his pension, but he had found a loophole. If he was to die before he was sixty, his life insurance would give Primrose a payout of £100,000 and she would receive a pension of £10,000 per year. However, if he died past the age of sixty, she wouldn't receive a large payout at all and would only get £5,000 per year as a pension. Some believe that this was his way of asserting control through his death. By killing himself now, Primrose would be looked after and he would have outsmarted the authorities again. In Shipman's mind, even in death – he had won.

There were mixed emotions over Shipman's death. Some were happy that he was dead and that we could forget about him, whereas others felt like he had taken the easy way out instead of paying penance for his crimes. By killing himself, there were questions that would never be answered. Why did he do it? How many people did he really kill? And would we have ever got a real confession from him? Some inmates have since said to the press that he had confessed to them and that the death toll is more likely to be around 500, but these stories are unverified and somewhat unlikely. A control freak like Shipman, who had never ever admitted that he was guilty of murder, or even forging Kathleen Grundy's will, would have been unlikely to give over that amount of control to an inmate. Psychologists who have studied Shipman and his pattern of behaviour believe that, even if he had lived, he never would have spoken out, he never would have confessed.

Chapter 15

Timeline

1946	Harold Frederick Shipman is born.
1949	Primrose May Oxtoby (Shipman's future wife) is born.
1963	Vera Shipman dies of lung cancer, Shipman is present at her death.
1965	Shipman enrols at Leeds University Medical School. Shipman meets Primrose Oxtoby. Primrose falls pregnant.
1966	The marriage of Harold Frederick Shipman and Primrose May Oxtoby.
1970	Shipman graduates from university with an MB. Shipman start his first job in medicine and a junior house officer at Pontefract General Infirmary.
1971	Shipman is registered with the General Medical Council Shipman's first son, Christopher, is born. Shipman gains a diploma in child health.
1971-4	Three suspicious deaths under Shipman's care included 4 year-old Susie Garfitt.
1974	Shipman gains a diploma in obstetrics and gynaecology. Shipman moves to Todmorden as an assistant GP at Abraham Ormerod Medical Practice. Shipman injects Elaine Oswald and almost kills her. Shipman begins to suffer blackouts and seizures due to pethidine addiction.
1975	Seven suspicious deaths noted, one later proved unlawful by the Shipman Inquiry. The Home Office look into Shipman's drug use. Shipman's partners discover his pethidine addiction and confront him; Shipman resigns and checks into rehab.
1976	Shipman pleads guilty to three separate drugs charges. Shipman signs an agreement that he won't work in general practice. Shipman starts work as in a medical administration job in Durham.
1977	Shipman moves to Hyde and starts at Donneybrook Practice as a GP.

1978	Nine suspicious deaths of which four are later deemed unlawful.
1979	Six suspicious deaths of which two are later deemed unlawful.
1980	One suspicious death noted.
1981	Six suspicious deaths of which two are later deemed unlawful.
1982	Four suspicious deaths noted.
1983	Three suspicious deaths of which two are later deemed unlawful.
1984	Thirteen suspicious deaths of which nine are later deemed unlawful.
1985	Fifteen suspicious deaths of which eleven are later deemed unlawful.
1986	Ten suspicious deaths of which eight are later deemed unlawful.
1987	Nine suspicious deaths of which eight are later deemed unlawful.
1988	Eleven unlawful deaths.
1989	Twelve unlawful deaths.
1990	Two unlawful deaths.
1991	Shipman leaves Donneybrook on bad terms after stealing patients and leaving his partners in debt.
1992	Shipman set up his own practice called 'The Surgery'.
1993	Seventeen suspicious deaths of which sixteen are later deemed unlawful. Shipman's patient's medical records become computerised.
1994	Thirteen suspicious deaths of which eleven are later deemed unlawful.
1995	Thirty-one suspicious deaths of which twenty-nine are later deemed unlawful and one resulted in a murder conviction.
1996	Thirty-one suspicious deaths of which twenty-seven are later deemed unlawful and three resulted in a murder conviction.
1997	Thirty-eight suspicious deaths of which thirty-two are later deemed unlawful and five resulted in a murder conviction.
1998	Seventeen unlawful killings of which six resulted in a murder conviction.

Shipman kills his last victim, Kathleen Grundy.
Shipman forges Kathleen Grundy's will.
Kathleen Grundy's body is exhumed.
Shipman is arrested for the murder of Kathleen Grundy.
Police search Shipman's house and office.
The exhumation of fourteen more bodies are authorized.
Toxicology results point to death by morphine overdose.
Shipman is charged with fifteen counts of murder.

1999   Shipman's trial begins at Preston Crown Court where he is
        accused of killing fifteen elderly patients and forging one
        will – Shipman pleads not guilty.

2000   Shipman is found guilty on all fifteen counts of murder and
        is sentenced to life in prison.
        Health Secretary, Alan Milburn, announces an inquiry into
        the circumstances surrounding the murders. The Inquiry is
        announced as private and causes public outcry.
        Police reveal that they are investigating 175 deaths, but that
        Shipman will not be charged with any more murders.
        Shipman is transferred to HMP Frankland.
        A court battle is won to make the Shipman Inquiry public.

2001   The Shipman Inquiry opens and is chaired by Dame
        Janet Smith.
        Over 400 suspicious cases are examined.

2002   The first stage of the report concludes that Shipman killed
        at least 215 of his patients in Hyde. Over the 215, 171 were
        women and 44 were men. The youngest victim was 47.

2003   Shipman is transferred to HMP Wakefield.
        The Shipman Inquiry calls for reforms in medical practice
        including monitoring of mortality rates and death
        certificates as well as more vigorous testing for GPs.
        Shipman is asked to take part in the inquiry, but refuses.
        Police interview Shipman about suspicious deaths in
        Todmorden, but he refuses to answer any questions.

2004   Shipman commits suicide.
        The Shipman Inquiry re-investigates suspicious death
        in Pontefract.

2005   The Shipman Report is published.

Chapter 16

Aftermath

Aftermath

After Shipman's trial, the Department of Health revealed their plans to make doctors disclose all previous criminal convictions, as well as any actions taken towards them by professional regulatory bodies, before they would be allowed to go on any medical lists. GPs also had to report any deaths and/or serious incidents that may have happened in their surgeries, and there was a review of the procedures concerning death certificates. There was also to be a full clinical audit of Shipman's past practice and this audit was conducted by Professor Richard Baker, of the University of Leicester.

The audit analysed data from Shipman's medical practice and compared it to other GP practices in the area, which had similar patient numbers on their books. The death rate of women over the age of sixty-five in the area was found to be 2.7%, but in Shipman's practice it was 26% - ten times that of the others. It was also found that 68% of Shipman's patients died in their own homes, whereas the average figure for the area was just 19%.

Shipman issued 449 death certificates when he worked in Hyde, more than double the highest figures from other practices. In Todmorden, the death rate for Shipman's patients was slightly higher than other GPs, but the deaths fitted the pattern of the murders Shipman had been convicted of. This discovery in the Baker report motivated police to undertake further investigations in Todmorden and an appeal for relatives and friends of the deceased were asked to come forward.

The audit initially found that Shipman may have been responsible for the deaths of at least 236 of his patients over twenty-four years. This was the first informed bid to try to measure the grand scale of the murders. Professor Baker concluded that there had been 265 murders, a closer figure to the one found in the later, public inquiry.

Shipman was considered to be a good doctor by the community he had served as a local GP. Although he could be difficult at times, it was believed that he was committed to his patients and was a completely competent doctor. There was, however, little evidence to be found about his worthiness to practice. He had a history of drug misuse and there had been complaints by some patients made against him, there doesn't seem to have been a way in which he had been assessed in order to establish his competence.

At his trial, Shipman was convicted of killing just fifteen people. This did give closure for those victims' families, but for the murders that he was not convicted for, the relatives were, as one family member is reported to have said, "left in limbo". There were too many unanswered questions, from missing effects after Shipman's victims had died to the 'what ifs' and 'if onlys' felt by grieving relatives, even questioning their own part in the events.

Between August 2000 and April 2001, twenty-seven inquests were held for, what the police considered to be, suspicious deaths. The coroner wrote to Harold Shipman twice asking him to participate in the inquests via a video link from prison, but he never received a reply. The coroner heard the same Shipman story over and over again, that patients refused hospital treatment, that they took ill on one of his visits, supposedly made telephone calls to ask for Shipman to call (calls that could not be traced). The coroner spoke against putting 'death by natural causes' onto a death certificate stating that this was not a cause of death. He was also appalled that a second doctor would readily agree to sign a cremation certificate, which gave natural causes as the cause of death. Furthermore, that a registrar didn't refer the deaths to the coroner he found incredible.

A full inquiry was called for by the families and friends of Shipman's victims so that they, too, could be given the complete recognition of what had happened to them at the hands of Harold Shipman. To their horror, the relatives discovered that the proposed inquiry, to be chaired by Lord Laming, would be held behind closed doors with no press or public access. Incensed by this, the relatives of fifty-five of the victims formed an action group and asked a solicitor, Ann Alexander, to act on their behalf in order to force the government to hold the inquiry in public. Backed by local and national newspapers, the Laming Inquiry was eventually scrapped and a full public inquiry began in June 2001. It would last almost two years and was chaired by a High Court Judge, Dame Janet Smith.

Dame Janet Smith was sixty when the inquiry began and she lived in Stockport, not far from most of the victims. The first decision she had to make was what the nature of the inquiry should be. She decided to investigate each suspicious death, and those that may have been suspicious, and came to a conclusion on each individual case. She said that there were hundreds of people who didn't know if their loved ones had died a natural death or been murdered. They needed to know the truth so that they could grieve properly.

The inquiry also looked into other things, such as the use of death certificates and cremation forms, how sudden deaths are investigated, disciplinary rules for doctors, how doctor's qualifications are recorded, and disclosure of any past criminal convictions, overseeing dispensing of controlled drugs (including how they are stored and disposed of) and monitoring death rates in practices. Once these had been investigated, recommendations could be made to improve systems and make changes so that patients had better protection.

The inquiry looked into 887 deaths in which Harold Shipman may have been involved in some way or other, if not directly. A decision was made on 493 cases; the other 394 could not have been caused by Shipman as the patient had either died in hospital, been out of the country, died in an accident or been alive a long time after Shipman's last visit to them.

Dame Janet decided to proceed with were those cases that were almost definitely down to foul play, or where the friends and relatives were deeply troubled by the circumstances of the deaths. The inquiry examined the records of 500 patients who died whilst Shipman was their doctor. Approximately 2,300 witness statements were taken from the police and a further 1370 by the inquiry. On top of this, there were documents from the coroner, medical records, cremation certificates, telephone records, diaries, etc. When they had been analysed, there were around 270,000 pages of evidence. The investigation cost £21 million.

At the beginning of the Inquiry, Dame Janet Smith told all the relatives and friends that if any of the deaths were, in fact, a Shipman murder, they would be given a new death certificate by the coroner, without them having to make a formal inquest.

The inquiry took on over thirty administrative staff and a vital part of the work done by them was to liaise with the Tameside Victim Support Team, led by Helen Ogborn. The team worked flat-out to support the relatives and was kept informed by the inquiry. When witnesses were contacted by the inquiry team, they sent out information about Victim Support. Helen Ogborn was awarded the MBE in the Queen's birthday honours list in 2003. She insisted that the award was really for everyone who helped in the Victim Support team and she held a party on the day of the presentation for all her co-workers.

Manchester Town Hall had been chosen as the best place for all the evidence to be heard as it was fairly close to Hyde. Cameras were trained onto whoever was speaking and their image projected onto two big screens and documents projected onto a third. These images, plus a sound feed, were also broadcast to the public library in Hyde, which gave people the opportunity to follow proceedings without having to travel to Manchester. For the first few days it proved to be very popular, but the spectators became less and less as time went on and a year after the inquiry began, the link to Hyde was closed down.

It had been decided from the onset that the inquiry was to be paper-free with documents being scanned and entered into a database and given a reference number. At the end of each day's proceedings, transcripts were posted onto the inquiry's website which had been set up by a Manchester company called 'Spoken Image'.

Once a month, the inquiry had to leave the council chamber where they were all housed to allow the council members to meet to discuss council issues. Every month, it took a day and a half to reinstall all the computers, so that the inquiry could continue.

Dame Janet consulted the friends and families of the victims about their feelings regarding the inquiry being broadcast on television or radio and they were all definitely against it. CNN (Cable News Network) put in a challenge and eventually Dame Janet agreed to them being allowed to televise the second phase of the inquiry, which must have been a disappointment as they were really interested in the first phase which looked into the deaths, and this is what they wanted to be able to film.

Witnesses arrived at the Town Hall where they were taken to a Witness Room. They could also listen to the proceedings from the public gallery. An inquiry like this is different from a court of law where witnesses are not allowed to hear earlier statements before giving their own. Volunteers from the Victim Support team were always present, especially when there was a lot of media interest. They were particularly needed when Primrose Shipman took the stand to give her evidence.

Primrose Shipman had supported her husband throughout his medical career and during his trial, where she had given evidence insisting on his innocence. The families of his victims were outraged when she repeatedly said she knew nothing of his alleged murders. A witness summons had to be served on her as she had refused to attend the inquiry to give evidence. This may have been because it had become apparent that she had been at the homes of two of the victims when they had died (Irene Chapman and Joyce Woodhead) and she had also been with her husband during the Elaine Oswald incident. Her lawyer then asked that she should be allowed to give her evidence in private or by a video link, thus protecting her from the public in the council chamber where the evidence was being given. Dame Janet refused, saying that she would not be at a disadvantage and would be able to speak in the accepted calm atmosphere that prevailed in the chamber. She said that Primrose Shipman was not accused of any wrongdoing and that she would be helping to piece together the information about her husband's activities. She would be treated with respect and if there was any intimidation then she would have the public gallery cleared. Dame Janet promised to protect Primrose from any possible harassment from lawyers during their questioning.

When Primrose gave her evidence, she knew that she could not be convicted of any criminal charges and anything she said could not be used against Harold Shipman in court either. This was providing she didn't give any false evidence, which would be pointless given that she was not liable to prosecution for telling the truth. For the victims' families, however, this felt like a get-out for Primrose.

She appeared to give evidence at the inquiry on Friday, 16th November 2001. There were only seventy seats in the public gallery and observers had queued up for them. Every single press seat was also taken. The anticipated outcome from Primrose's evidence was expected to explain Shipman's crimes and many thought that there was no way she could have lived with him without knowing what had been going on. Unfortunately the victims' relatives were bitterly disappointed, as throughout the morning, when she was asked questions, she was heard to mutter, "I can't remember," or, "I don't know," or, I'm not sure," and said she was, "so confused." These statements were repeated over and over. She also denied taking two rings from Irene Chapman after her death. Andrew Spink, the lawyer acting on behalf of the victims' families, tried very hard to persuade Primrose to give up her information. He asked her if she was convinced of Shipman's innocence. She said she was. He also asked her if she was doing everything she could to help Shipman's solicitors in bringing in an appeal. Again, she confirmed that she was. At this point Dame Janet intervened and stopped his questions as Primrose was close to tears. The relatives disagreed and had said that her giving evidence had been a complete waste of time. This was the only time that Primrose had been questioned. She had never been interviewed by the police, as they had never had enough evidence. Shipman was still controlling his wife from his prison cell; he had groomed her so well that whatever she had said at the inquiry was worthless. Dame Janet had described Primrose as 'a straightforward and honest witness' because before giving her evidence, Primrose had been asked if she still had any documents relevant to the investigation. She said she had handed them all over. These documents were three boxes of records found at the Donneybrook surgery and included Shipman's visit books. Dame Janet said that had she been dishonest, she would have held on to them to protect her husband, or maybe even destroyed them.

After giving evidence, Primrose left 'by the back door'. She was taken to a private car park from where she departed in the back of a dark-blue car, which sped down a one-way street in the wrong direction.

Professor Elaine Oswald travelled from Tennessee, USA, to give evidence about when Shipman had given her an injection which had almost killed her. After she had given her evidence, Caroline Swift, leading counsel to the inquiry, was critical of Oswald; she said that Oswald had rehearsed what she was going to say until she was word perfect and portrayed someone playing a part. The inquiry decided that she had, indeed, been assaulted by Shipman, but Elaine Oswald felt she had been badly treated. She said she had been made to feel as if she were the one on trial and wished she had been given the same consideration as Primrose Shipman had. The Shipman Inquiry published what became known as 'The Numbers' on the 19th July 2002. This was the first time that Harold Frederick Shipman had been known to be responsible for 215 deaths, plus another forty-five suspicious deaths. The First Report of six volumes weighed fourteen pounds and the friends and families of the victims knew for certain, for the first time, that Harold Shipman had murdered their loved ones, usually in the afternoon and mostly when he had called unannounced. Many newspapers ran the headline: 'Death in the Afternoon'.

The second and third reports of the inquiry were published in July 2003, a year after the first report. The second had looked into the failed police investigation and the third into Death Certificates and investigations of deaths by coroners. It made some strong recommendations for a change in the system of certifying deaths.

The fourth report was published in July 2004, another year on, and was about rules governing controlled drugs. The fifth report followed in December 2004 and had looked into the safeguarding of patients, including whistle-blowing when colleagues have serious concerns or worrying suspicions.

On the 24th January 2005, Dame Janet Smith issued her sixth, and final, report of the inquiry. She said that she believed that the probable number of Shipman's victims between 1971 and 1998 was, in fact, 250. A total of 459 people died whilst Shipman was their doctor, but it is not known exactly how many were his victims, as he was the only doctor to issue the death certificate.

The enormity of Shipman's murderous activities meant that he was infamous and went from being a British doctor who killed some of his patients to the most prolific serial killer the world has known. Whilst the investigations were being carried out, Shipman stayed at Durham Prison, still maintaining his innocence, and was staunchly defended by his wife and his family. He was moved to Wakefield Prison in June 2003, which made visits from his family easier.

When Harold Shipman hanged himself, using bed sheets, in his cell at Wakefield Prison on 13th January 2004, the day before his 58th birthday, some of his victims' families said they had felt cheated as they would never now be able to hear his confession, if he were ever to make one, and find out why he committed so many murders. They would never have closure.

On hearing the news of Shipman's suicide, the Home Secretary, David Blunkett is reported to have said: "You wake up and you receive a call telling you Shipman has topped himself and you think, is it too early to open a bottle? And then you discover that everybody's very upset that he's done it."

Some British tabloids ran celebratory stories at his suicide and openly encouraged other serial killers to follow suit. The Sun's headline read: 'Ship Ship hooray!' Others referred to him as a 'cold coward' (Daily Mirror) and berated the prison service for allowing the suicide to take place at all.

The reason Shipman committed suicide was never found out, but he had apparently told his probation officer that he was considering it so as Primrose could receive an NHS pension, even though he had been struck off and denied his own pension. She did receive a full NHS pension, which she would not have done had he reached the age of 60. She needed this as she couldn't work and had been condemned and shunned for being the wife of a notorious serial killer. She would never have been able to start a new life and she had nothing. Shipman had taken it all from her and she was being punished for his evil doing.

Primrose had stood by her husband, protesting his innocence even though he had been belligerent with his family. She had supported him when he set up his own practice, even offering to be his receptionist. When Primrose rang the surgery to tell him that the other members of the family were sitting down to dinner, Shipman would tell her, "Nobody eats until I get there."

Like Shipman, Primrose was thought well of in the local community. She would child-mind her neighbours' children who trusted her with them implicitly. She was not, however, a good housewife and the home was dirty. She was kind and people accepted her, saying, "Her heart was in the right place."

In prison, Shipman had been encouraged to attend courses, which could have led to him confessing his guilt, but he refused to attend. He then became tearful and emotional when his privileges were removed, including being able to telephone his wife from the prison. These privileges were returned the week before he took his own life. Shipman's ex-cellmate, Tony Fleming, said that Primrose had written to her husband asking him to, "tell her everything, no matter what." Perhaps Primrose was having doubts about her husband and may have suspected his guilt as well.

Primrose Shipman may have been suffering from a rare psychological condition called "Folie A Deux". This is where two people in a close relationship share a psychosis where the stronger one makes the weaker one accept their deceptions as normal. Harold Shipman may have conditioned his barely literate wife into believing his own fanciful notions and this made her his greatest ally.

In 2005, it was discovered that Harold Shipman may have stolen from his victims. In 1998, police found over £10,000 worth of jewellery hidden in Shipman's garage. In March 2005, police wrote to the families of Shipman's victims to ask them to identify the jewellery. The unidentified pieces were handed to the Assets Recovery Agency and sixty-six pieces returned to Primrose Shipman, but thirty-three were not hers and were sent for auction, the proceeds going to Tameside Victim Support. Only one piece of jewellery could be returned to a murdered patient's family – this was a diamond ring and they were able to supply a photograph as proof of ownership.

Primrose, too, had become a victim of Shipman's pathological reign of terror and killing, as did his children. He ended their lifestyle and she moved to a small cottage near Wetherby, using her denial of his crimes and proclaiming his innocence as a way of hiding her shame. Shipman left Primrose, and his children, Sara, 36, Christopher, 32, David, 24, and Sam, 21, a legacy they can never escape from – a man convicted of fifteen murders and believed to have committed as many as 250 more. Some of the children completed their university courses, but it would have been a tough time for them. Even though they had taken new identities, being the children of a psychopathic murderer would be difficult to live with. Shipman's family had to face the world's condemnation for the rest of their lives – they received the life sentence he avoided.

Six doctors were also charged with misconduct by the General Medical Council, who said they should have seen patterns forming between Shipman's home visits and the subsequent deaths of his patients. All six doctors were found not guilty.

Another hearing was held in October 2005 against two doctors who worked at Tameside General Hospital in 1994. They had failed to recognise that Shipman had deliberately given an excessive overdose of morphine.

A 2005 inquiry into Shipman's suicide found that it, "could not have been predicted or prevented, but that procedures should nonetheless be re-examined."

It can only be hoped that never again will someone as unrepentant as Harold Shipman walk this earth, but his conviction of the murders and the changes brought about by the inquiry can be testament to the 250+ innocent people who he murdered without remorse.

A memorial garden to Shipman's victims, called the Garden of Tranquillity, opened in Hyde Park, Hyde on the 30 July 2005; it honours the victims of Britain's most prolific serial killer.

Picture Credits